Editorial project:
© 2023 **booq** publishing, S.L.
c/ Domènech, 7-9, 2º 1ª
08012 Barcelona, Spain
T: +34 93 268 80 88
www.booqpublishing.com

ISBN: 978-84-9936-644-9 [EN]
ISBN: 978-84-9936-633-3 [DE]
ISBN: 978-84-9936-632-6 [ES]

© Éditions du Layeur
Dépôt Légal : septembre 2023
Espagne, en septembre 2023

ISBN : 978-2-38378-041-0

Editorial coordinator:
Claudia Martínez Alonso

Art director:
Mireia Casanovas Soley

Editor:
Daniela Santos Quartino

Layout:
Cristina Simó Perales

Translation:
© **booq** publishing, S.L.

Printing in Spain

As a pioneer of the 21st century in his own territory, the new ruralite pursues the ideal of the promised land and the reconquest of infinite spaces. This promise is based on a paradoxical symbiosis between nature and technology, the internet and telecommuting.

Modern life makes many people feel suffocated in the city where they do not feel satisfied, in terms of costs, square metres, quality of life. They flee from environmental degradation, stress and depersonalisation. In the urban environment, going to the countryside has always been an ideal escape to a better life.

Today, architects and designers are turning that yearning into reality with buildings that are rooted in tradition, but respond to the more demanding requirements of modern life. They are set in landscapes dominated by greenery and panoramic views, on farms or agricultural land. They have plenty of space inside and outside the dwellings, more comfort, more connection to the outdoors and more light. Some architects deliberately choose farmhouse aesthetics, others are inspired by vernacular architecture, and some use modern geometries.

Whether they are new constructions or renovations of old structures, the rural residences presented in this book are located in different parts of the world. They promote sustainability and are closely intertwined with local geography and culture.

Many of these buildings are year-round homes and workplaces, where their inhabitants find a balance between work and personal life. Others function as retreats for peace and reconnection with the land, offering a sanctuary for those who want a break from the hustle and bustle of the city and to immerse themselves in the serenity of nature.

Als Pionier des 21. Jahrhunderts auf ihrem eigenen Territorium verfolgt der neue „Ruralita" das Ideal vom gelobten Land und der Rückeroberung der unendlichen Räume. Dieses Versprechen basiert auf einer paradoxen Symbiose zwischen Natur und Technologie, Internet und Fernarbeit.

Das moderne Leben führt dazu, dass viele Menschen sich in der Stadt erstickt fühlen, wo sie nicht zufrieden sind aufgrund der Kosten, der Quadratmeterzahl und der Lebensqualität. Sie fliehen vor Umweltverschmutzung, Stress und Entfremdung. Auf dem Land zu leben war schon immer ein idealer Fluchtweg in ein besseres Leben in städtischer Umgebung.

Heutzutage verwirklichen Architekten und Designer diesen Wunsch mit Konstruktionen, die in der Tradition verwurzelt sind, aber den anspruchsvollsten Anforderungen des modernen Lebens gerecht werden. Sie sind in Landschaften mit viel Grün und Panoramablick auf Bauernhöfen oder landwirtschaftlichen Flächen platziert. Sie bieten viel Platz sowohl drinnen als auch draußen, mehr Komfort, eine stärkere Verbindung zu Außenbereichen und mehr Licht. Einige Architekten wählen bewusst die Ästhetik des Bauernhofs, andere lassen sich von der einheimischen Architektur inspirieren, und wieder andere nutzen moderne Geometrien.

Ob es sich um Neubauten oder Renovierungen alter Strukturen handelt, die ländlichen Residenzen in diesem Buch befinden sich an verschiedenen Orten auf der Welt. Sie fördern Nachhaltigkeit und sind eng mit Geografie und lokaler Kultur verbunden.

Viele dieser Konstruktionen sind das ganze Jahr über Wohn- und Arbeitsstätten, in denen die Bewohner ein Gleichgewicht zwischen Arbeit und Privatleben finden. Andere dienen hingegen als Orte des Friedens und der Wiederanbindung an die Erde, indem sie einen Zufluchtsort für diejenigen bieten, die eine Pause vom Trubel der Stadt suchen und sich in der Ruhe der Natur verlieren möchten.

Pionnier du XXIᵉ siècle sur son propre territoire, le nouveau rural poursuit l'idéal de la terre promise et de la reconquête des espaces infinis. Cette promesse repose sur une symbiose paradoxale entre nature et technologie, Internet et télétravail.

La vie moderne fait que beaucoup de gens se sentent étouffés dans la ville où ils ne se sentent pas satisfaits, en termes de coûts, de mètres carrés, de qualité de vie. Ils fuient la dégradation de l'environnement, le stress et la dépersonnalisation. Dans l'environnement urbain, aller à la campagne a toujours été une échappatoire idéale vers une vie meilleure.

Aujourd'hui, les architectes et les concepteurs transforment cette aspiration en réalité avec des bâtiments qui sont enracinés dans la tradition, mais qui répondent aux exigences plus élevées de la vie moderne. Elles sont implantées dans des paysages dominés par la verdure et les vues panoramiques, sur des fermes ou des terres agricoles. Elles offrent beaucoup d'espace à l'intérieur et à l'extérieur des habitations, plus de confort, plus de lien avec l'extérieur et plus de lumière. Certains architectes choisissent délibérément l'esthétique de la ferme, d'autres s'inspirent de l'architecture vernaculaire, d'autres encore utilisent des géométries modernes.

Qu'il s'agisse de nouvelles constructions ou de rénovations d'anciennes structures, les résidences rurales présentées dans ce livre sont situées dans différentes parties du monde. Elles favorisent la durabilité et sont étroitement liées à la géographie et à la culture locales.

Nombre de ces bâtiments sont des habitations et des lieux de travail ouverts toute l'année, où leurs habitants trouvent un équilibre entre vie professionnelle et vie personnelle. D'autres fonctionnent comme des retraites pour la paix et la reconnexion avec la terre, offrant un sanctuaire à ceux qui veulent faire une pause dans l'agitation de la ville et s'immerger dans la sérénité de la nature.

Como pionero del siglo XXI en su propio territorio, el nuevo ruralita persigue el ideal de la tierra prometida y la reconquista de los espacios infinitos. Esta promesa se basa en una simbiosis paradójica entre la naturaleza y la tecnología, Internet y el trabajo a distancia.

La vida moderna hace que muchas personas se sienten sofocados en la ciudad donde no están satisfechas, por costes, metros cuadrados, calidad de vida. Huyen del deterioro medioambiental, el estrés y la despersonalización. En el medio urbano, irse al campo siempre ha sido un ideal de escape hacia una mejor vida.

Hoy en día, arquitectos y diseñadores están haciendo realidad ese anhelo con construcciones que se arraigan en la tradición, pero responden a las más exigentes demandas de la vida moderna. Están emplazadas en paisajes dominados por el verde y las vistas panorámicas, en fincas o terrenos agrícolas. Tienen mucho espacio dentro y fuera de las viviendas, mayor confort, mayor conexión con las áreas exteriores y más luz. Algunos arquitectos eligen deliberadamente la estética de la granja, otros se inspiran en la arquitectura vernácula y hay quienes recurren a las geometrías modernas.

Ya sean construcciones nuevas o renovaciones de estructuras antiguas, las residencias rurales que se presentan en este libro están situadas en diferentes partes del mundo. Promueven la sostenibilidad y están estrechamente entrelazadas con la geografía y la cultura local.

Muchas de estas construcciones son hogares y lugares de trabajo durante todo el año, donde sus habitantes encuentran un equilibrio entre vida laboral y personal. Otras, en cambio, funcionan como retiros de paz y reconexión con la tierra, ofreciendo un santuario para aquellos que quieren una pausa al ajetreo de la ciudad y sumergirse en la serenidad de la naturaleza.

Established in 2006, Aaron Neubert Architects is an architecture and design firm renowned for crafting captivating spaces that artfully blend landscape, light, and materials, elevating the human experience while prioritizing environmental conservation. Under the leadership of Aaron Neubert, FAIA, the firm boasts an extensive portfolio encompassing museums, hotels, private residences, multi-family housing, and restaurants, all thoughtfully designed with a strong emphasis on sustainability and environmentally-conscious principles. The firm's innovative strategies have proven successful in preserving delicate ecosystems and contributing positively to the well-being of the communities they serve, earning them acclaim in global publications and recognition through prestigious awards and international exhibitions at esteemed universities and design events.

Aaron Neubert Architects wurde 2006 gegründet und ist ein Architektur- und Designbüro, das für die Gestaltung fesselnder Räume bekannt ist, in denen Landschaft, Licht und Materialien kunstvoll miteinander verschmelzen, um die menschliche Erfahrung zu steigern und gleichzeitig die Umwelt zu schützen. Unter der Leitung von Aaron Neubert, FAIA, verfügt das Büro über ein umfangreiches Portfolio, das Museen, Hotels, Privatwohnungen, Mehrfamilienhäuser und Restaurants umfasst, die alle mit Bedacht und unter Berücksichtigung von Nachhaltigkeit und umweltbewussten Prinzipien entworfen wurden. Die innovativen Strategien des Unternehmens haben sich als erfolgreich erwiesen, wenn es darum geht, empfindliche Ökosysteme zu bewahren und einen positiven Beitrag zum Wohlbefinden der Gemeinden zu leisten, denen sie dienen. Dies brachte dem Unternehmen Beifall in internationalen Publikationen und Anerkennung durch prestigeträchtige Preise und internationale Ausstellungen an angesehenen Universitäten und Designveranstaltungen ein.

AARON NEUBERT ARCHITECTS/ANX

AARON NEUBERT, FAIA

a-n-x.com

Fondé en 2006, Aaron Neubert Architects est un cabinet d'architecture et de design qui crée des espaces attrayants, fusionnant le paysage, la lumière et les matériaux pour améliorer l'expérience humaine et promouvoir la conservation de l'environnement. Dirigé par Aaron Neubert, FAIA, le cabinet dispose d'un vaste portefeuille qui comprend des musées, des hôtels et des résidences privées, des logements collectifs et des restaurants, et met l'accent sur la durabilité et la conception respectueuse de l'environnement. Ses stratégies innovantes préservent les écosystèmes fragiles tout en favorisant le bien-être de la communauté. Le cabinet a fait l'objet d'articles dans des publications de premier plan dans le monde entier. Son travail a été récompensé par des prix prestigieux et a fait l'objet d'expositions internationales dans des universités et lors d'événements liés à la conception.

Fundado en 2006, Aaron Neubert Architects es un estudio de arquitectura y diseño que crea espacios atractivos, fusionando paisaje, luz y materiales, para mejorar la experiencia humana y promover la conservación del medio ambiente. Dirigido por Aaron Neubert, FAIA, el estudio cuenta con un extenso portafolio que abarca museos, hoteles y residencias privadas, viviendas plurifamilares y restaurantes, con un enfoque puesto en la sostenibilidad y el diseño adaptado al entorno. Sus estrategias innovadoras preservan ecosistemas delicados a la vez que benefician el bienestar de la comunidad. La firma ha sido destacada en reconocidas publicaciones a nivel mundial. Su trabajo ha recibido prestigiosos premios y ha sido exhibido internacionalmente en universidades y eventos de diseño.

ARROYO OAK HOUSE

Castaic, California, United States

Photos © Brian Thomas Jones

Looking to shorten their work commute, a Southern California-based couple sought a residence closer to their manufacturing facility. They acquired a picturesque site characterized by sandstone topography, intersected by a dry river, and adorned with abundant native vegetation. Enlisting the expertise of ANX, a house with an open, transparent structure was designed to harmoniously blend with the semi-arid landscape, maximizing natural light and scenic vistas. The residence was carefully crafted with a series of interconnected pavilions of varying dimensions, giving rise to gardens, terraces, and decks that seamlessly intertwine indoor and outdoor spaces. The house's exterior is clad in zinc, cedar, and limestone. Inside, the home spans two levels, achieving seamless integration between the domestic space and the rural environment, utilizing cedar and limestone as primary finish materials. Outside, the pool terrace and outdoor living room merge with the meadow and stream, creating a delightful natural circuit for leisurely strolls. Given the area's susceptibility to fires, the landscaping and irrigation system were meticulously designed with specific features to ensure environmental safety and preservation.

Ein Ehepaar aus Südkalifornien war auf der Suche nach einem Wohnsitz in der Nähe seiner Firma, um den Arbeitsweg zu verkürzen. Sie erwarben ein malerisches Grundstück mit Sandsteintopographie, einer trockenen Flussüberquerung und üppiger einheimischer Vegetation. Die Eigentümer beauftragten ANX mit der Planung eines Hauses mit offener, transparenter Struktur, das sich harmonisch in die halbtrockene Landschaft einfügt und das natürliche Licht und den Panoramablick optimal nutzt. Das Haus besteht aus einer Reihe miteinander verbundener Pavillons unterschiedlicher Größe, die zu Gärten, Terrassen und Decks führen, welche die Innen- und Außenbereiche nahtlos miteinander verbinden. Das Äußere des Hauses ist mit Zink, Zedernholz und Kalkstein verkleidet. Im Inneren erstreckt sich das Haus über zwei Ebenen, wobei eine sehr gute Integration zwischen dem Wohnbereich und der ländlichen Umgebung erreicht wurde und Zedernholz und Kalkstein als Hauptausstattungsmaterialien verwendet wurden. Im Außenbereich verschmelzen die Poolterrasse und das Wohnzimmer mit der Landschaft und dem Bach, so dass ein attraktiver natürlicher Rundweg für gemütliche Spaziergänge entsteht. Angesichts der Brandgefahr in diesem Gebiet wurden die Landschaftsgestaltung und das Bewässerungssystem sorgfältig geplant, um die Sicherheit und den Schutz der Umwelt zu gewährleisten.

Les propriétaires, un couple du sud de la Californie, cherchaient une résidence plus proche de leur entreprise afin de réduire leurs déplacements. Ils ont acquis un site attrayant avec une rivière asséchée et une végétation indigène abondante, et se sont tournés vers l'expertise d'ANX. Le projet qui en résulte est une maison ouverte et transparente intégrée dans le paysage semi-aride, tirant parti de la lumière naturelle et des vues panoramiques. Il s'agit d'une série de pavillons interconnectés de différentes tailles, menant à des jardins, des terrasses et des ponts qui entremêlent les espaces intérieurs et extérieurs. L'extérieur de la maison est revêtu de zinc, de cèdre et de pierre calcaire. À l'intérieur, la maison est répartie sur deux niveaux, ce qui permet une très bonne intégration entre l'espace domestique et l'environnement rural. La terrasse de la piscine et le salon se fondent dans le paysage, créant un circuit naturel attrayant pour des promenades tranquilles. Compte tenu de la vulnérabilité de la région aux incendies, l'aménagement paysager et le système d'irrigation ont été conçus avec des caractéristiques spécifiques pour assurer la sécurité et la préservation de l'environnement.

Los propietarios, una pareja del sur de California buscaban una residencia más cercana a su empresa para acortar los desplazamientos por trabajo. Para ello adquirieron un atractivo emplazamiento atravesado por un río seco y abundante vegetación autóctona, y acudieron a la experiencia de ANX. El diseño resultante es una casa de estructura abierta y transparente, integrada en el paisaje semiárido, que aprovecha la luz natural y las vistas panorámicas. Se trata de una serie de pabellones interconectados de distintas dimensiones, que dan lugar a jardines, terrazas y cubiertas que entrelazan los espacios interiores y exteriores. El exterior de la casa está revestido de zinc, cedro y piedra caliza. En el interior, la vivienda se extiende en dos niveles, logrando una muy buena integración entre el espacio doméstico y el entorno rural. La terraza de la piscina y el salón se funden con el paisaje creando un atractivo circuito natural para paseos tranquilos. Dada la susceptibilidad de la zona a los incendios, el paisajismo y el sistema de riego se diseñaron con características específicas para garantizar la seguridad y la preservación del medio ambiente.

Section

1. Entry
2. Kitchen
3. Deck
4. Lap pool
5. Bedroom
6. Deck

Architect, designer, artist, and entrepreneur, Ben Albury was born in Melbourne, Australia, and has lived in New York for 15 years. He has 25 years of experience as an architect in the building and construction industry on three continents. He has worked at various scales in a variety of areas including residential, commercial, civic, institutional, hospitality, retail and mixed-use.

Ben founded Amalgam Studio LLC in 2013, a New York-based multidisciplinary practice incorporating architecture, interiors and product design work, with a focus on sustainable residential design. He is also the founder of Venhaus LLC in 2018, a venture to explore the possibilities of energy efficient modular and family home design.

Der Architekt, Designer, Künstler und Unternehmer Ben Albury wurde in Melbourne (Australien) geboren und lebt seit 15 Jahren in New York. Er verfügt über 25 Jahre Erfahrung als Architekt im Bauwesen und Bauindustrie auf drei Kontinenten. Er hat in verschiedenen Bereichen wie Wohn-, Gewerbe-, Zivil-, Institutionen-, Gastgewerbe-, Einzelhandels- und Mischnutzungsbereichen in unterschiedlichen Maßstäben gearbeitet.

Ben gründete 2013 das Amalgam Studio LLC, ein multidisziplinäres Atelier mit Sitz in New York, das Architektur-, Innenarchitektur- und Produktdesignarbeiten mit besonderem Fokus auf nachhaltigem Wohnungsdesign vereint. Im Jahr 2018 gründete er auch die Firma Venhaus LLC, um die Möglichkeiten des Designs energieeffizienter, modularen Familienhäuser zu erkunden.

AMALGAM STUDIO

BEN ALBURY

amalgam-studio.com

Architecte, designer, artiste et entrepreneur, Ben Albury est né à Melbourne, en Australie, et vit à New York depuis 15 ans. Il a 25 ans d'expérience en tant qu'architecte dans le secteur du bâtiment et de la construction sur trois continents. Il a travaillé à différentes échelles dans des domaines aussi variés que le résidentiel, le commercial, le civique, l'institutionnel, l'hôtellerie, le commerce de détail et l'utilisation mixte.

Ben a fondé Amalgam Studio LLC en 2013, un cabinet multidisciplinaire basé à New York qui intègre des travaux d'architecture, d'intérieurs et de conception de produits, en mettant l'accent sur la conception résidentielle durable. Il est également le fondateur de Venhaus LLC en 2018, une entreprise visant à explorer les possibilités de conception de maisons modulaires et familiales économes en énergie.

Arquitecto, diseñador, artista, y emprendedor, Ben Albury nació en Melbourne (Australia), y vive en Nueva York desde hace 15 años. Cuenta con 25 años de experiencia como arquitecto en el sector de la edificación y la construcción en tres continentes. Ha trabajado a distintas escalas en diversas áreas, como la residencial, comercial, cívico, institucional, hostelera, minorista y de uso mixto.

Ben fundó Amalgam Studio LLC en 2013, un taller multidisciplinar con sede en Nueva York, que incorpora trabajos de arquitectura, interiores y diseño de productos, con especial atención al diseño residencial sostenible. También es el fundador de Venhaus LLC en 2018, una empresa para explorar las posibilidades del diseño de casas familiares y modulares energéticamente eficientes.

SILVERNAILS

Hudson Valley, New York, United States

Photos © Oliver Mint & Jesse Turnquist

This wood and stone family residence sits atop a hill in the heart of the Hudson Valley. It is a weekend home designed to be easily converted into a permanent residence. Inspired by the rural setting, Amalgam Studio designed a long, linear barn-like main building and a secondary building around an open field and pool. The main residence features spacious rooms, vaulted ceilings with exposed timber beams, natural light and deliberately framed landscapes. Historic barn archetypes helped define the roof form, interior planning and overall massing. Exposed structures, high ceilings, lofts, large sliding glass doors and the use of natural stone in the basement walls were also inspirational.
Architect Ben Albury describes the house as "modern vernacular". Modern in terms of open planning, energy efficiency, materials and contemporary aesthetics. While vernacular is associated with the form, visual language and construction methodology of traditional and local architecture.

Diese Familienresidenz aus Holz und Stein liegt auf dem Gipfel eines Hügels im Herzen des Hudson Valley. Es handelt sich um ein Wochenendhaus, das leicht in einen dauerhaften Wohnsitz umgewandelt werden kann. Inspiriert von der ländlichen Umgebung entwarf das Amalgam Studio ein langes, lineares Hauptgebäude in Scheunenform und ein Nebengebäude umgeben von einem offenen Feld und einem Pool.
Das Hauptgebäude verfügt über geräumige Zimmer, gewölbte Decken mit sichtbaren Holzbalken, natürliches Licht und bewusst gerahmte Landschaften. Die Archetypen historischer Scheunen halfen dabei, die Dachform, die Innenplanung und die Gesamtmasse zu definieren. Auch sichtbare Strukturen, hohe Decken, Galerien, große Glastüren und der Einsatz von Naturstein in den Kellerwänden dienten als Inspiration.
Der Architekt Ben Albury beschreibt das Haus als „moderne Volksarchitektur". Modern in Bezug auf offene Grundrisse, Energieeffizienz, Materialien und zeitgenössische Ästhetik. Während „Volksarchitektur" mit der Form, der visuellen Sprache und der Bautechnik der traditionellen und lokalen Architektur assoziiert wird.

Cette résidence familiale en bois et en pierre se trouve au sommet d'une colline au cœur de la vallée de l'Hudson. Il s'agit d'une maison de week-end conçue pour être facilement convertie en résidence permanente. Inspiré par le cadre rural, Amalgam Studio a conçu un bâtiment principal long et linéaire, semblable à une grange, et un bâtiment secondaire autour d'un champ ouvert et d'une piscine.
La résidence principale se caractérise par des pièces spacieuses, des plafonds voûtés avec des poutres en bois apparentes, la lumière naturelle et des paysages délibérément encadrés. Les archétypes de granges historiques ont contribué à définir la forme du toit, l'aménagement intérieur et la volumétrie générale. Les structures exposées, les hauts plafonds, les lofts, les grandes portes vitrées coulissantes et l'utilisation de la pierre naturelle dans les murs du sous-sol ont également été une source d'inspiration.
L'architecte Ben Albury décrit la maison comme « vernaculaire moderne ». Moderne en termes de planification ouverte, d'efficacité énergétique, de matériaux et d'esthétique contemporaine. Le vernaculaire est associé à la forme, au langage visuel et à la méthodologie de construction de l'architecture traditionnelle et locale.

Esta residencia familiar de madera y piedra, se asienta en la cima de una colina en el corazón del Hudson Valley. Se trata de una casa de fin de semana diseñada para convertirse fácilmente en una residencia permanente. Inspirado en el entorno rural, Amalgam Studio diseñó una edificación principal larga y lineal en forma de granero, y otra secundaria, alrededor de un campo abierto y una piscina.
La residencia principal cuenta con habitaciones espaciosas, techos abovedados con vigas de madera a la vista, luz natural y paisajes deliberadamente enmarcados. Los arquetipos de los graneros históricos ayudaron a definir la forma del tejado, la planificación interior y la masa total. También han servido de inspiración las estructuras vistas, los techos altos, los altillos, las grandes puertas correderas de cristal y el uso de piedra natural en los muros del sótano.
El arquitecto Ben Albury, describe la casa como «moderna vernácula». Moderna en lo que se refiere a la planificación abierta, la eficiencia energética, los materiales y la estética contemporánea. Mientras que lo vernacular se asocia a la forma, el lenguaje visual y la metodología de construcción de la arquitectura tradicional y local.

Founded in Madrid in 2009, Arquitectura ALDESCUBIERTO is composed of Cristina Manene Roca, Fernando Orte García and Omar Miranda García. The studio has excelled in the development of architecture, interior design and landscaping projects. In 2020, they received the COAM interior design award for the Rehabilitation of housing in the Historic Centre of Fuencarral, and in 2022, the COACM Architecture Award for New Housing Works for Villa Icaria. The work of Arquitectura ALDESCUBIERTO focuses on residential research and landscape interventions. Their work, scattered throughout Spain, is characterised by establishing a close relationship with the environment, the careful selection of materials, the incorporation of natural lighting and a meticulous study of construction details. The members of the studio define themselves as practitioners of sincere, high quality architecture.

Gegründet 2009 in Madrid besteht Arquitectura ALDESCUBIERTO aus Cristina Manene Roca, Fernando Orte García und Omar Miranda García. Das Studio hat sich auf Architektur-, Innenarchitektur- und Landschaftsprojekte spezialisiert. Im Jahr 2020 erhielten sie den COAM-Preis für Innenarchitektur für die Renovierung eines Wohnhauses in der historischen Altstadt von Fuencarral und 2022 den COACM-Preis für Architektur für ein neues Wohnhaus namens Villa Icaria. Die Arbeit von Arquitectura ALDESCUBIERTO konzentriert sich auf Forschung im Bereich Wohnen und Interventionen in der Landschaft. Ihre Werke, die über die gesamte spanische Geografie verteilt sind, zeichnen sich durch eine enge Beziehung zur Umgebung, sorgfältige Auswahl der Materialien, Einbeziehung von natürlichem Licht und eine genaue Untersuchung der konstruktiven Details aus. Die Mitglieder des Studios bezeichnen sich selbst als Praktizierende einer ehrlichen und qualitativ hochwertigen Architektur.

ARQUITECTURA ALDESCUBIERTO

FERNANDO ORTE GARCÍA, CRISTINA MANENE ROCA, OMAR MIRANDA GARCÍA

arquitecturaldescubierto.com

Fondé à Madrid en 2009, Arquitectura ALDESCUBIERTO est composé de Cristina Manene Roca, Fernando Orte García et Omar Miranda García. Le studio excelle dans le développement de projets d'architecture, d'intérieurs et d'aménagement paysager. En 2020, ils ont reçu le prix COAM de design d'intérieur pour la rénovation d'une maison dans le centre historique de Fuencarral, et en 2022, le prix COACM d'architecture de nouveaux logements pour Villa Icaria. Le travail d'Arquitectura ALDESCUBIERTO se concentre sur la recherche résidentielle et les interventions paysagères. Leur travail, dispersé dans toute l'Espagne, se caractérise par l'établissement d'une relation étroite avec l'environnement, la sélection minutieuse des matériaux, l'incorporation de l'éclairage naturel et l'étude méticuleuse des détails de la construction. Les membres du studio se définissent comme des praticiens d'une architecture sincère et de haute qualité.

Fundado en Madrid en el año 2009, Arquitectura ALDESCUBIERTO está integrado por Cristina Manene Roca, Fernando Orte García y Omar Miranda García. El estudio se ha destacado en el desarrollo de proyectos de arquitectura, interiores y paisajismo. En 2020, recibieron el premio COAM de interiorismo por la Rehabilitación de vivienda en el Casco Histórico de Fuencarral, y en 2022, el Premio COACM de Arquitectura Obra Nueva Vivienda por Villa Icaria. El trabajo de Arquitectura ALDESCUBIERTO se enfoca en la investigación en el ámbito residencial y en las intervenciones en el paisaje. Su obra, dispersa por toda la geografía española, se caracteriza por establecer una estrecha relación con el entorno, la cuidadosa selección de materiales, la incorporación de iluminación natural y un minucioso estudio de los detalles constructivos. Los integrantes del estudio se definen a sí mismos como practicantes de una arquitectura sincera y de alta calidad.

VILLA ICARIA

Alcarria, Guadalajara, Spain

Photos © Imagen Subliminal

Villa Icaria seeks to establish a new relationship between the countryside and the city. This personal project of a family of architects is located in a territory of pine forests, olive groves and lavender fields, bathed by reservoirs and crossed by the Tagus River.

Like a small articulated village, the floor plan of the building is organised around two courtyard-plazas. Each volume generates a different type of space, some of which become caves in which to take refuge without losing the connection with the surroundings, and others are open areas which act as a visual transition between different areas of the garden. An infinity pool connects the garden and the house with the river, creating a continuous plane of turquoise water typical of the area. The dining room acts as a threshold between the access courtyard and the pool. The large table designed by Bruno Mathsson on the basis of the super-ellipse in the 1960s stands out. Ecological methods, local materials and local masons were used for the construction. The exposed concrete vaults, the rustic rendering of the interior walls and the polished concrete floors are in keeping with rural logic.

Die Villa Icaria strebt nach einer neuen Beziehung zwischen Land und Stadt. Dieses persönliche Projekt einer Architektenfamilie befindet sich in einer Landschaft mit Pinienwäldern, Oliven- und Lavendelfeldern, umgeben von Stauseen und vom Fluss Tajo durchzogen.

Wie ein kleines Dorf ist der Grundriss des Gebäudes um zwei Innenhöfe-Plätze angeordnet. Jedes Gebäudevolumen schafft eine Art Raumtypologie, einige werden zu Höhlen, in denen man Schutz suchen kann, ohne die Verbindung zur Umgebung zu verlieren, und andere sind offene Bereiche, die als visuelle Übergänge zwischen verschiedenen Gartenbereichen fungieren. Ein Infinity-Pool verbindet den Garten und das Haus mit dem Fluss und schafft eine durchgehende Ebene türkisfarbenen Wassers, typisch für die Region. Das Esszimmer fungiert als Schwelle zwischen dem Zugangshof und dem Pool. Besonders hervorzuheben ist der große Tisch, der in den 1960er Jahren von Bruno Mathsson entworfen wurde und auf der Superellipse basiert. Bei der Konstruktion wurden ökologische Methoden, lokale Materialien und örtliche Handwerker verwendet. Die sichtbaren Betondecken, die rustikale Verputztechnik der Innenwände und die polierten Betonböden entsprechen den Logiken des Ländlichen.

La Villa Icaria cherche à établir une nouvelle relation entre la campagne et la ville. Ce projet personnel d'une famille d'architectes est situé dans un territoire de forêts de pins, d'oliveraies et de champs de lavande, baigné par des réservoirs et traversé par le fleuve Tage.

Tel un petit village articulé, le plan du bâtiment s'organise autour de deux cours-plazas. Chaque volume génère un type d'espace différent, certains devenant des grottes dans lesquelles on peut se réfugier sans perdre le lien avec l'environnement, d'autres étant des espaces ouverts qui servent de transition visuelle entre les différentes zones du jardin. Une piscine à débordement relie le jardin et la maison à la rivière, créant un plan continu d'eau turquoise typique de la région. La salle à manger fait office de seuil entre la cour d'entrée et la piscine. La grande table conçue par Bruno Mathsson sur la base de la super-ellipse des années 1960 est remarquable. Des méthodes écologiques, des matériaux locaux et des maçons locaux ont été utilisés pour la construction. Les voûtes en béton apparent, l'enduit rustique des murs intérieurs et les sols en béton poli s'inscrivent dans une logique rurale.

Villa Icaria busca establecer una nueva relación entre campo y ciudad. Este proyecto personal de una familia de arquitectos se encuentra en un territorio de bosques de pinos, y campos de olivos y lavandas, bañado de embalses y atravesado por el río Tajo.

Como un pequeño pueblo articulado, la planta del edificio se organiza en torno a dos patios-plazas. Cada volumen genera una tipología de espacio, algunos se convierten en cuevas donde refugiarse sin perder la conexión con el entorno, y otros son zonas al descubierto que funcionan como transición visual entre distintas zonas del jardín. Una piscina de efecto infinito conecta el jardín y la casa con el río, creando un plano continuo de agua turquesa típica de la zona. El comedor funciona como umbral entre el patio de acceso y la piscina. Destaca la gran mesa diseñada por Bruno Mathsson a partir de la súper-elipse en los años 60. Para la construcción se usaron métodos ecológicos, materiales de la zona y albañiles locales. Las bovedillas vistas de hormigón, los enfoscados rústicos de las paredes interiores y los suelos de hormigón pulido responden a las lógicas de lo rural.

Arthouse Architects is an award-winning practice with offices in Nelson, Christchurch and Blenheim. Jorgen Andersen, Rachel Dodd and their highly dedicated and experienced team of 23 collaborate enthusiastically to create elegant and timeless solutions for projects of any scale. Their focus is on creating enduring designs.
The studio, founded in 2000, stands out for its commitment to creating spaces that combine aesthetic beauty with energy efficiency, all within a local context. The firm's projects have won NZIA Architectural Awards, Master Builders Awards and Commercial Building Awards in New Zealand.

Arthouse Architects ist ein preisgekröntes Studio mit Büros in Nelson, Christchurch und Blenheim. Jorgen Andersen, Rachel Dodd und ihr hochengagiertes und erfahrenes Team von 23 Personen arbeiten begeistert zusammen, um elegante und zeitlose Lösungen für Projekte jeder Größenordnung zu schaffen. Ihr Fokus liegt auf der Schaffung beständiger Designs.
Das im Jahr 2000 gegründete Studio zeichnet sich durch sein Engagement für die Schaffung von Räumen aus, die ästhetische Schönheit und Energieeffizienz miteinander verbinden, immer im lokalen Kontext. Die Projekte des Studios wurden mit dem NZIA Architectural Awards, den Master Builders Awards und den Commercial Building Awards in Neuseeland ausgezeichnet.

ARTHOUSE ARCHITECTS

JORGEN ANDERSEN, RACHEL DODD

arthousearchitects.co.nz

Arthouse Architects est un cabinet primé qui possède des bureaux à Nelson, Christchurch et Blenheim. Jorgen Andersen, Rachel Dodd et leur équipe de 23 personnes très dévouées et expérimentées collaborent avec enthousiasme pour créer des solutions élégantes et intemporelles pour des projets de toute envergure. Ils s'attachent à créer des designs pérennes.
Le studio, fondé en 2000, se distingue par son engagement à créer des espaces qui allient beauté esthétique et efficacité énergétique, le tout dans un contexte local. Les projets de l'entreprise ont été récompensés par des prix d'architecture NZIA, des prix Master Builders et des prix Commercial Building en Nouvelle-Zélande

Arthouse Architects es un galardonado estudio con oficinas en Nelson, Christchurch y Blenheim. Jorgen Andersen, Rachel Dodd y su equipo de 23 personas, altamente dedicados y experimentados, colaboran con entusiasmo para crear soluciones elegantes y atemporales en proyectos de cualquier escala. Su enfoque se centra en la creación de diseños perdurables.
El estudio, fundado en el año 2000, se destaca por su compromiso de crear espacios que combinan la belleza estética con la eficiencia energética, todo dentro de un contexto local. Los proyectos de la firma han sido galardonados por el programa NZIA Architectural Awards, Master Builders Awards y Commercial Building Awards en Nueva Zelanda.

VINEYARD HOUSE

Blenheim, South Island, New Zealand

Photos © Sarah Rowlands

The project is a modern and welcoming house that meets the clients' needs for a spacious family home with views over vineyards and hills. It is a farmhouse with two wings from a hidden central entrance. The bedrooms are angled eastwards from a central entry point which allows light to enter. The day area, on the other hand is staggered to include two outdoor spaces that are exposed to the sun and sheltered from the wind.
Inside the house, the robust concrete elements are softened by the handcrafted oak joinery. The exterior is wrapped in dark stained cedar and precast fair-faced concrete panels. The roofline slopes upwards to respond to the winter sun, adding a dynamic aesthetic.
The concrete floors and walls offer excellent thermal capacity to absorb heat during the winter and release it at night when the temperature drops. During the summer, this same thermal capacity allows heat to be absorbed. A line of windows close to the roof, as well as well positioned doors and windows, promote natural cross ventilation.

Das Projekt ist ein modernes und gemütliches Haus, das den Bedürfnissen der Kunden nach einem geräumigen Familienheim mit Blick auf die Weinberge und Hügel gerecht wird. Es handelt sich um eine Farm mit zwei Flügeln, die von einem verborgenen zentralen Eingang ausgehen. Die Schlafzimmer befinden sich im Ostflügel, der viel Licht hereinlässt. Der Tagesbereich erstreckt sich in gestaffelter Form über zwei Außenbereiche, die den Sonnenverlauf erkennen und vor Wind schützen.
Im Inneren des Hauses werden robuste Betonelemente durch handwerkliche Eichenholzarbeiten aufgeweicht. Die Außenfassade ist mit dunkel getöntem Zedernholz und vorgefertigten Sichtbetonplatten verkleidet. Die Dachlinie ist nach oben geneigt, um auf die Winter-sonne zu reagieren und eine dynamische Ästhetik hinzuzufügen.
Die Betonböden und -wände bieten eine ausgezeichnete Wärmekapazität, um im Winter Wärme aufzunehmen und während der Nacht abzugeben, wenn die Temperatur abfällt. Im Sommer ermöglicht diese thermische Masse die Aufnahme von Hitze. Eine Reihe von Oberlichtern in der Nähe des Dachs sowie gut platzierte Türen und Fenster fördern die natürliche Querlüftung.

Le projet est une maison moderne et accueillante qui répond aux besoins des clients pour une maison familiale spacieuse avec vue sur les vignobles et les collines. Il s'agit d'une ferme avec deux ailes à partir d'une entrée centrale cachée. Les chambres à coucher sont logées sur le côté est, qui laisse entrer la lumière. La zone de jour, quant à elle, est décalée pour englober deux espaces extérieurs à partir desquels il est possible de reconnaître le soleil et de se protéger du vent.
À l'intérieur de la maison, les éléments robustes en béton sont adoucis par la menuiserie en chêne fabriquée à la main. L'extérieur est enveloppé de cèdre teinté foncé et de panneaux préfabriqués en béton apparent. La ligne de toit s'incline vers le haut pour répondre au soleil d'hiver, ajoutant une esthétique dynamique.
Les sols et les murs en béton offrent une excellente capacité thermique pour absorber la chaleur en hiver et la restituer la nuit lorsque la température baisse. En été, cette même capacité thermique permet d'absorber la chaleur. Une ligne de fenêtres près du toit, ainsi que des portes et des fenêtres bien placées, favorisent la ventilation transversale naturelle.

El proyecto es una casa moderna y acogedora que cumple con las necesidades de los clientes de tener un amplio hogar familiar con vistas a los viñedos y las colinas. Se trata de una granja con dos alas a partir de una entrada central oculta. Los dormitorios se alojan en el lado Este, lo que permite la entrada de luz. La zona de día, por su parte, se escalona para abarcar dos áreas exteriores desde las que se reconoce el paso del sol y se protege de los vientos.
En el interior de la vivienda, los elementos robustos de hormigón se suavizan con la carpintería artesanal de roble. El exterior está envuelto en cedro teñido de oscuro, y paneles prefabricados de hormigón visto. La línea del tejado se inclina hacia arriba para responder al sol de invierno, añadiendo una estética dinámica.
Los suelos y paredes de hormigón ofrecen una excelente capacidad térmica para absorber el calor durante el invierno y liberarlo durante la noche, cuando la temperatura disminuye. Durante el verano, esta misma capacidad térmica permite absorber el calor. Una línea de ventanas cerca del techo, además de puertas y ventanas bien posicionadas, favorecen la ventilación cruzada natural.

Barlis Wedlick is known for designing expressive, sustainable and characterful spaces. With a focus on precision and a deep connection to the landscape, his collaborative process creates projects that combine highly crafted design with responsible construction. Over the past 20 years, Barlis Wedlick has created a long portfolio of projects, including private residences, affordable housing and sustainable commercial complexes. The firm is led by Alan Barlis, an accomplished architect with a Master of Architecture degree from MIT and chartered in several states. In 2018, he was inducted into the American Institute of Architects College of Fellows for his work and teaching in sustainable design. He is a Professor of High Performance Architecture at the City College of New York and a member of the American Institute of Architects Committee on the Environment.

Barlis Wedlick ist bekannt für den Entwurf ausdrucksstarker, nachhaltiger und charaktervoller Räume. Mit einem Schwerpunkt auf Präzision und einer tiefen Verbindung zur Landschaft schafft ihr kollaborativer Prozess Projekte, die hochentwickeltes Design mit verantwortungsbewusstem Bau kombinieren. In den letzten 20 Jahren hat Barlis Wedlick eine umfangreiche Projektpalette entwickelt, die private Residenzen, bezahlbaren Wohnraum und nachhaltige Gewerbekomplexe umfasst. Das Unternehmen wird von Alan Barlis geleitet, einem renommierten Architekten mit einem Master-Abschluss in Architektur vom MIT und Zulassungen in mehreren Bundesstaaten. 2018 wurde er als Fellow des American Institute of Architects College of Fellows für seine Arbeit und Lehrtätigkeit im Bereich nachhaltiges Design aufgenommen. Er ist Professor für Performance Architecture am City College of New York und Mitglied des Umweltausschusses des American Institute of Architects.

BARLIS WEDLICK

ALAN BARLIS

barliswedlick.com

Barlis Wedlick est connu pour la conception d'espaces expressifs, durables et de caractère. En mettant l'accent sur la précision et un lien profond avec le paysage, son processus de collaboration permet de créer des projets qui combinent une conception hautement artisanale et une construction responsable. Au cours des 20 dernières années, Barlis Wedlick a créé un long portefeuille de projets, notamment des résidences privées, des logements abordables et des complexes commerciaux durables. Le cabinet est dirigé par Alan Barlis, un architecte accompli, titulaire d'un master en architecture du MIT et agréé dans plusieurs États. En 2018, il a été intronisé au Collège des membres de l'American Institute of Architects pour son travail et son enseignement dans le domaine de la conception durable. Il est professeur d'architecture haute performance au City College de New York et membre du comité de l'environnement de l'American Institute of Architects.

Barlis Wedlick es conocido por diseñar espacios expresivos, sostenibles y con carácter. Con un enfoque en la precisión y una profunda conexión con el paisaje, su proceso de colaboración crea proyectos que combinan un diseño altamente elaborado con una construcción responsable. En los últimos 20 años, Barlis Wedlick ha creado una larga cartera de proyectos, que incluye residencias privadas, viviendas asequibles y complejos comerciales sostenibles. La firma está dirigida por Alan Barlis, arquitecto de reconocida trayectoria con un Máster en Arquitectura por el MIT y colegiado en varios Estados. En 2018, fue admitido en el American Institute of Architects College of Fellows por su trabajo y labor docente en el diseño sostenible. Es profesor de Arquitectura de Alto Rendimiento en el City College de Nueva York y miembro del Comité de Medio Ambiente del Instituto Americano de Arquitectos.

MEADOW HOUSE

Westchester County, New York, United States

Photos © Conor Harrigan, Peter Aaron, Rob Cardillo

This house is the fruit of the dreams of the client, a fashion executive, who longed for a sustainable space that would provide him with peace and well-being, away from his daily routine. Inspired by the barns of yesteryear, the design rescued the ruined structures of the old property to give it new functions.
The 350 m² building consists of three connected L-shaped volumes with large windows that look out onto the property's original barn, forming an interior courtyard. The historic barn was restored by local specialists and converted into an event and performance space.
The interior of the house combines modern touches with unique vintage pieces. Wood and sand tones predominate. The owner took care of the décor to achieve a bespoke look inspired by his work in menswear.
A garden with elaborate rustic-style landscaping defines the exteriors of this coastal California home. It is completed by a swimming pool for the summer seasons, making this property the ultimate retreat for calm and relaxation.

Dieses Haus ist das Ergebnis der Vision des Kunden, eines Modemagnaten, der sich nach einem nachhaltigen Raum sehnte, der ihm Ruhe und Wohlbefinden fernab seines hektischen Alltags bietet. Inspiriert von alten Scheunen, wurden die verfallenen Strukturen des ehemaligen Anwesens für neue Zwecke wiederverwendet.
Das 350 m² große Gebäude besteht aus drei L-förmig angeordneten und miteinander verbundenen Volumen mit großen Fenstern, die auf die ursprüngliche Scheune des Anwesens blicken und einen Innenhof bilden. Lokale Fachleute wurden damit beauftragt, die historische Scheune zu restaurieren und in einen Veranstaltungs- und Ausstellungsraum umzuwandeln.
Das Innere des Hauses kombiniert moderne Elemente mit einzigartigen Vintage-Stücken. Holz und sandige Töne dominieren. Der Eigentümer kümmerte sich um die Dekoration, um einen maßgeschneiderten Look zu erreichen, der von seiner Arbeit in der Männermode inspiriert ist. Ein Garten mit aufwendig gestalteten rustikalen Landschaftsgestaltungen prägt die Außenbereiche dieses Hauses an der kalifornischen Küste. Ein Pool vervollständigt das Anwesen und macht es zum ultimativen Rückzugsort für Ruhe und Entspannung.

Cette maison est le fruit de la vision du client, un cadre du secteur de la mode, qui aspirait à un espace durable lui apportant paix et bien-être, loin de sa routine quotidienne. Inspiré par les granges d'antan, le projet a sauvé les structures en ruine de l'ancienne propriété pour lui donner de nouvelles fonctions.
Le bâtiment de 350 m² se compose de trois volumes en forme de « L » reliés entre eux, avec de grandes fenêtres qui donnent sur la grange d'origine de la propriété, formant ainsi une cour intérieure. La grange historique a été restaurée par des spécialistes locaux et transformée en espace d'événements et de spectacles.
L'intérieur de la maison allie des touches modernes à des pièces vintage uniques. Les tons bois et sable prédominent. Le propriétaire s'est occupé de la décoration pour obtenir un look sur mesure inspiré de son travail dans le domaine de la mode masculine.
Un jardin avec un aménagement paysager élaboré de style rustique définit les extérieurs de cette maison de la côte californienne. Il est complété par une piscine pour les saisons estivales, faisant de cette propriété le lieu de retraite ultime pour le calme et la détente.

Esta casa es el fruto de la visión del cliente, un ejecutivo del sector de la moda, que anhelaba un espacio sostenible que le brindara tranquilidad y bienestar, alejado de su rutina diaria. Inspirado en los graneros de antaño, el diseño rescató las estructuras en ruinas de la antigua propiedad para darle nuevas funciones.
La construcción de 350 m² consta de tres volúmenes dispuestos en «L» y conectados, con grandes ventanales que miran hacia el granero original de la propiedad, formando un patio interior. Especialistas locales se encargaron de restaurar el granero histórico y lo convirtieron en un espacio para eventos y espectáculos.
El interior de la casa combina toques modernos con piezas vintage únicas. Predomina la madera y los tonos arenas. El propietario se encargó de la decoración para conseguir un aspecto a medida inspirado en su trabajo en la moda masculina.
Un jardín con elaborados diseños paisajísticos de estilo rústico define los exteriores de esta vivienda en la zona costera de California. Lo completa una piscina para las épocas estivales, lo que convierte a esta propiedad en el refugio definitivo para la calma y la relajación.

Charlottesville-based Bushman Dreyfus Architects was born with the intention of merging the agility of a small firm with the knowledge and experience of a larger entity. From modest beginnings, the studio has gradually grown, starting with a project for a charity auction: an elegant steel aviary. Their success led them to win a competition to design a public amphitheater in Charlottesville.

Bushman Dreyfus Architects' speciality lies in design, where their primary focus is on clarity of communication and consensus building. In addition to architecture, the studio's designers bring a diversity of cultural and community interests, which enriches their work and allows them to incorporate exciting perspectives.

Bushman Dreyfus Architects mit Sitz in Charlottesville wurde mit dem Ziel gegründet, die Agilität einer kleinen Organisation mit dem Wissen und der Erfahrung einer größeren Einheit zu vereinen. Von bescheidenen Anfängen aus hat sich das Studio allmählich weiterentwickelt, angefangen mit einem Projekt für eine Wohltätigkeitsauktion: einem eleganten Stahlvogelhaus. Ihr Erfolg führte dazu, dass sie einen Wettbewerb gewannen, um ein öffentliches Amphitheater in Charlottesville zu entwerfen.

Die Spezialität von Bushman Dreyfus Architects liegt im Design, wobei ihr Hauptaugenmerk auf klarer Kommunikation und Konsensfindung liegt. Neben Architektur bringen die Designer des Studios eine Vielfalt an kulturellen und gemeindlichen Interessen mit ein, was ihre Arbeit bereichert und ihnen ermöglicht, aufregende Perspektiven einzubeziehen.

BUSHMAN DREYFUS ARCHITECTS

JEFF BUSHMAN, JEFF DREYFUS, LISA MORAN, TIM TESSIER

bdarchitects.com

Bushman Dreyfus Architects, basé à Charlottesville, est né avec l'intention de fusionner l'agilité d'une petite organisation avec les connaissances et l'expérience d'une entité plus importante. Après des débuts modestes, le studio s'est progressivement développé, en commençant par un projet pour une vente aux enchères caritative : une élégante volière en acier. Leur succès les a conduits à remporter un concours pour la conception d'un amphithéâtre public à Charlottesville.

La spécialité de Bushman Dreyfus Architects réside dans la conception, où l'accent est mis sur la clarté de la communication et la recherche d'un consensus. Outre l'architecture, les concepteurs du cabinet apportent une diversité d'intérêts culturels et communautaires, ce qui enrichit leur travail et leur permet d'intégrer des perspectives passionnantes.

Con sede en Charlottesville, Bushman Dreyfus Architects nace con la intención de fusionar la agilidad de una organización pequeña con el conocimiento y la experiencia de una entidad más grande. Desde sus modestos inicios, el estudio ha ido creciendo gradualmente, comenzando con un proyecto para una subasta benéfica: una elegante pajarera de acero. Su éxito les llevó a ganar un concurso para diseñar un anfiteatro público en Charlottesville.

La especialidad de Bushman Dreyfus Architects radica en el diseño, donde su enfoque principal es la claridad en la comunicación y la búsqueda del consenso. Además de la arquitectura, los diseñadores del estudio aportan una diversidad de intereses culturales y comunitarios, lo que enriquece su trabajo y les permite incorporar perspectivas emocionantes.

HEIRLOOM FARM STUDIO

Virginia, United States

Photos © Virginia Hamrick Photography

This studio was custom-designed for an artist in search of inspiration, in a community committed to sustainable living. Set on a farm, with the majestic Blue Ridge Mountains as a backdrop, the studio is located on an elevated point of land, surrounded by pastures, an orchard and a farmhouse.

The building's structure is simple and minimalist in form, inspired by Scandinavian vernacular-style barns that have stood the test of time. As one approaches the building, the dark geometry resolves itself into individual wooden slats. The colour palette is absolutely minimalist, with the poplar slats stained dark for both the wall and the roof. The wood is heat-treated for durability.

The interior is an open-plan space, painted white. It is equipped with adjustable track lighting in the ceiling and a spacious storage cupboard. Large windows illuminate the room from three sides and offer a 270-degree view of the surrounding meadows and mountains, and the dynamic shadows of the adjacent mature oak trees.

Dieses Studio inmitten der Natur wurde maßgeschneidert für einen Künstler, der nach Inspiration sucht, in einer Gemeinschaft, die sich für nachhaltige Produktion einsetzt. Das Studio befindet sich auf einem Bauernhof, mit den majestätischen Blue Ridge Mountains im Hintergrund und ist an einer erhöhten Stelle des Geländes gelegen, umgeben von Wiesen, einem Obstgarten und einem Bauernhaus.

Die Struktur des Gebäudes ist schlicht und minimalistisch, inspiriert von skandinavischen Scheunen im traditionellen Stil, die die Zeit überdauert haben. Wenn man sich dem Gebäude nähert, verwandelt sich die dunkle Geometrie in einzelne Holzlatten. Die Farbpalette ist absolut minimalistisch, mit dunkel gefärbten Pappelholzlatten für die Wand und das Dach.

Das Holz ist thermisch behandelt für eine längere Haltbarkeit. Das Innere ist ein offener, weiß gestrichener Raum. Es ist mit dimmbarer Schienenbeleuchtung an der Decke und einem geräumigen Schrank zur Aufbewahrung von Materialien ausgestattet. Die großen Fenster erhellen den Raum von drei Seiten und bieten einen 270-Grad-Blick auf die umliegenden Wiesen und Berge sowie die dynamischen Schatten der angrenzenden alten Eichen.

Ce studio en pleine nature a été conçu sur mesure pour un artiste en quête d'inspiration, au sein d'une communauté engagée dans la production durable. Situé dans une ferme, avec les majestueuses Blue Ridge Mountains en toile de fond, le studio se trouve sur un terrain surélevé, entouré de prairies, d'un verger et d'une ferme.

La structure du bâtiment est simple et minimaliste, inspirée des granges scandinaves de style vernaculaire qui ont résisté à l'épreuve du temps. À mesure que l'on s'approche du bâtiment, la géométrie sombre se résout en lamelles de bois individuelles. La palette de couleurs est absolument minimaliste, les lattes de peuplier étant teintées en foncé pour les murs et le toit. Le bois est traité à la chaleur pour une meilleure durabilité.

L'intérieur est un espace ouvert, peint en blanc. Il est équipé d'un éclairage sur rail réglable au plafond et d'un grand placard de rangement. De grandes fenêtres éclairent la pièce sur trois côtés et offrent une vue à 270 degrés sur les prairies et les montagnes environnantes, ainsi que sur les ombres dynamiques des chênes matures adjacents.

Este estudio en plena naturaleza se diseñó a medida para un artista en busca de inspiración, en una comunidad comprometida con la producción sostenible. Ubicado en una granja, con las majestuosas Blue Ridge Mountains como telón de fondo, el estudio está emplazado en un punto elevado del terreno, rodeado de prados, un huerto y una casa de campo.

La estructura del edificio es de forma sencilla y minimalista, inspirada en los graneros escandinavos de estilo vernáculo, que han resistido la prueba del tiempo. A medida que uno se acerca a la edificación, la geometría oscura se resuelve en listones individuales de madera. La paleta de colores es absolutamente minimalista, con los listones de álamo teñidos de oscuro tanto para la pared como para el tejado. La madera está tratada térmicamente para una mayor duración.

El interior es un espacio diáfano, pintado de blanco. Está equipado con iluminación de riel regulable en el techo y un espacioso armario para guardar los materiales. Los grandes ventanales iluminan la sala desde tres lados y ofrecen una vista de 270 grados de los prados y montañas circundantes, y las sombras dinámicas de los robles maduros adyacentes.

West elevation

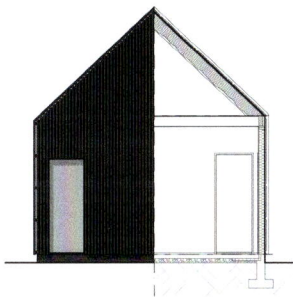

North elevation

East elevation

South elevation

Since its founding in 1985 by Lewis W Butler, San Francisco based Butler Armsden Architects has been the premier residential architecture firm for clients seeking quality design and performance homes. Heading the firm now, Federico Engel, Glenda Flaim and Chandra Campbell are carrying on the ideals of the founder. The firm's projects emerge from deep collaboration with the clients and the exchange of ideas. Most of its work is in San Francisco or the surrounding Bay Area counties.

The studio's work focuses on the optimal use of materials, architectural form, space and light to design iconic homes that blend into their sites and neighbourhoods. The studio's award-winning projects are diverse in nature and have appeared in publications ranging from Architectural Digest to the Wall Street Journal.

Seit seiner Gründung im Jahr 1985 durch Lewis W. Butler ist das in San Francisco ansässige Architekturbüro Butler Armsden Architects das führende Architekturbüro für Kunden, die hochwertiges Design und leistungsfähige Häuser suchen. Federico Engel, Glenda Flaim und Chandra Campbell, die das Büro jetzt leiten, führen die Ideale des Gründers fort. Die Projekte des Büros entstehen in enger Zusammenarbeit mit den Kunden und durch den Austausch von Ideen. Der Großteil der Arbeit findet in San Francisco oder den umliegenden Bezirken der Bay Area statt.

Die Arbeit des Büros konzentriert sich auf die optimale Nutzung von Materialien, architektonischen Formen, Raum und Licht, um ikonische Häuser zu entwerfen, die sich in ihre Standorte und Stadtviertel integrieren. Die preisgekrönten Projekte des Büros sind vielfältig und wurden in Publikationen von Architectural Digest bis hin zum Wall Street Journal vorgestellt.

BUTLER ARMSDEN ARCHITECTS

LEWIS W. BUTLER, CHELSEA EDGERTON, FEDERICO ENGEL, GLENDA FLAIM, CHANDRA CAMPBELL, DAVE STURM

butlerarmsden.com

Depuis sa création en 1985 par Lewis W. Butler, Butler Armsden Architects est le premier cabinet d'architecture résidentielle pour les clients à la recherche d'un design de qualité et de logements performants. Federico Engel, Glenda Flaim et Chandra Campbell, qui dirigent aujourd'hui le cabinet basé à San Francisco, perpétuent les idéaux du fondateur. Leurs projets sont le fruit d'une étroite collaboration avec leurs clients. La plupart de leurs travaux se déroulent à San Francisco ou dans les comtés environnants de la région de la Baie.

Le travail du studio se concentre sur l'utilisation optimale des matériaux, de la forme architecturale, de l'espace et de la lumière pour concevoir des maisons emblématiques qui s'intègrent à leur site et à leur quartier. Les projets primés du studio sont de nature diverse et ont été publiés dans des revues telles que l'Architectural Digest ou le Wall Street Journal.

Desde que fue fundada en 1985 por Lewis W. Butler, Butler Armsden Architects, ha sido la principal firma de arquitectura residencial para clientes que buscan un diseño de calidad y viviendas de alto rendimiento. Federico Engel, Glenda Flaim y Chandra Campbell, que dirigen en la actualidad la empresa con sede en San Francisco, mantienen los ideales del fundador. Sus proyectos surgen de una profunda colaboración con los clientes. La mayor parte de su trabajo se desarrolla en San Francisco o en los condados circundantes de Bay Area.

El trabajo del estudio se orienta hacia el uso óptimo de los materiales, las formas arquitectónicas, el espacio y la luz, para diseñar casas icónicas que se integran en sus emplazamientos y barrios. Los galardonados proyectos del estudio son de diversa índole y han aparecido en publicaciones que van desde Architectural Digest al Wall Street Journal.

POINT REYES RESIDENCE

Point Reyes Station, California, United States

Photos © David Duncan Livingston

Environmental concerns have been key to the owners, activists and residents in San Francisco. They asked Project Manager Dave Sturm and Chelsea Edgerton to design the house they would move into permanently. The architectural style combines contemporary elements with traditional forms, such as gable roofs. All rooms face out towards the sea and the captivating surroundings. To ensure that the views are expanded, large steel-framed windows were installed.
Inside, the design follows a minimalist approach with clean lines and understated aesthetics inspired by architect Luis Barragan. Cubic shelving is seamlessly recessed into the walls, and hardware-free doors pivot elegantly to provide privacy. The organic palette includes oak floors and cream-coloured plaster walls, which complement the furnishings and artwork.
One of the biggest challenges of the project was to resolve both outdoor privacy and fire resistance. The landscaping design favoured the use of indigenous plants.

Umweltbelange waren für die Eigentümer, Aktivisten und Anwohner in San Francisco ausschlaggebend, als sie Projektmanager Dave Sturm und Chelsea Edgerton baten, das Haus zu entwerfen, in das sie dauerhaft einziehen würden.
Der architektonische Stil kombiniert zeitgenössische Elemente mit traditionellen Formen wie Satteldächern. Alle Räume sind zum Meer und zur faszinierenden Umgebung ausgerichtet. Um den Blick zu maximieren, wurden große Fenster mit Stahlrahmen installiert.
Im Inneren folgt das Design einem minimalistischen Ansatz mit klaren Linien und schlichter Ästhetik, inspiriert von Architekt Luis Barragán. Die kubischen Regale sind nahtlos in die Wände eingelassen, und die grifflosen Türen schwingen elegant zur Gewährleistung von Privatsphäre. Die organische Farbpalette umfasst Eichenböden und cremefarbene Gipswände, die Möbel und Kunstwerke ergänzen.
Eine der größten Herausforderungen des Projekts bestand darin, gleichzeitig Privatsphäre im Freien und Feuerbeständigkeit zu gewährleisten. Das Landschaftsdesign setzt auf einheimische Pflanzen.

Les préoccupations environnementales ont été au cœur des préoccupations des propriétaires, des militants et des habitants de San Francisco, qui ont demandé au chef de projet Dave Sturm et à Chelsea Edgerton qui conçoivent la maison dans laquelle ils allaient s'installer de façon permanente.
Le style architectural associe des éléments contemporains à des formes traditionnelles, telles que les toits à pignon. Toutes les pièces sont orientées vers la mer et l'environnement captivant. De grandes fenêtres à cadre en acier ont été installées afin de maximiser la vue.
À l'intérieur, le design suit une approche minimaliste avec des lignes épurées et une esthétique discrète inspirée par l'architecte Luis Barragan. Les étagères cubiques sont parfaitement encastrées dans les murs et les portes sans quincaillerie pivotent élégamment pour préserver l'intimité. La palette organique comprend des sols en chêne et des murs en plâtre de couleur crème, qui complètent le mobilier et les œuvres d'art.
L'un des plus grands défis du projet était d'assurer à la fois l'intimité extérieure et la résistance au feu. L'aménagement paysager a opté pour l'utilisation de plantes indigènes.

La preocupación por el medio ambiente ha sido clave para que los propietarios, activistas y residentes en San Francisco, hayan pedido a al Project Manager Dave Sturm y a Chelsea Edgerton que diseñen la casa a la que se mudarían de forma permanente.
El estilo arquitectónico combina elementos contemporáneos con formas tradicionales, como los tejados a dos aguas. Todas las habitaciones están orientadas hacia el mar y el cautivador entorno. Para asegurar maximizar las vistas, se instalaron grandes ventanales con marcos de acero.
En el interior, el diseño sigue un planteamiento minimalista de líneas limpias y la estética sobria inspiradas en el arquitecto Luis Barragán. Las estanterías cúbicas se empotran perfectamente en las paredes, y las puertas sin herrajes pivotan con elegancia para proporcionar intimidad. La paleta orgánica incluye suelos de roble y paredes de yeso color crema, que complementan el mobiliario y las obras de arte.
Uno de los mayores retos del proyecto fue resolver a la vez la privacidad en el exterior con la resistencia al fuego. El diseño paisajístico se decantó por el uso de plantas autóctonas.

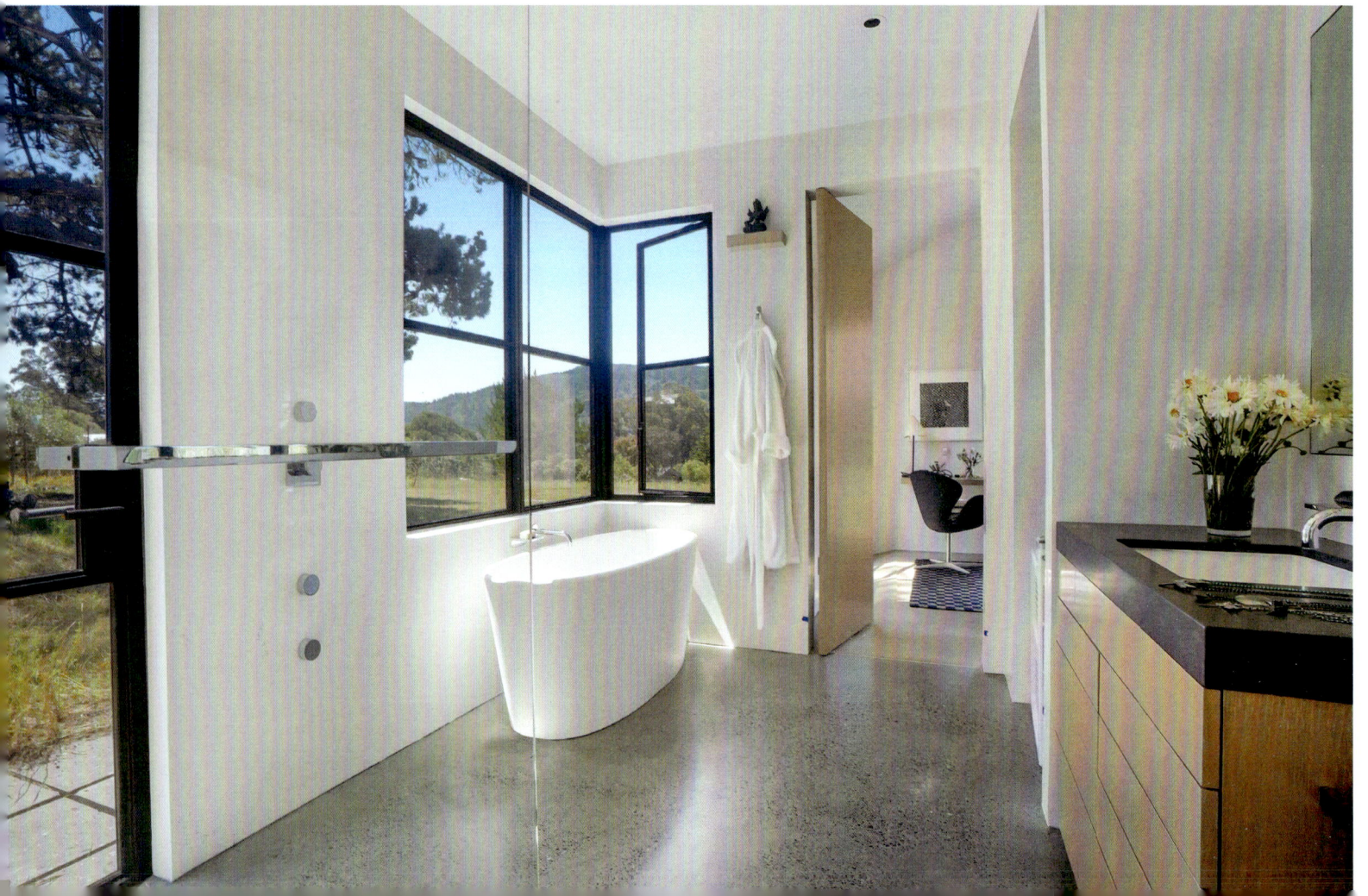

Led by Nicholas Byrne and a dedicated creative team, Byrne Architects is renowned for projects where iconic structures are seamlessly integrated with landscape, technology and interior design.
From boutique hotels to fine dining restaurants, dynamic workspaces to luxury residential projects, the Melbourne-based firm encompasses a wide range of design projects.
The studio has won accolades for its work, and has received numerous awards for its projects, such as the Balmoral Beach House. They are committed to delivering exceptional architectural experiences that exceed their clients' expectations and enhance the beauty and functionality of each space.

Unter der Leitung von Nicholas Byrne und einem spezialisierten kreativen Team ist Byrne Architects bekannt für Projekte, bei denen ikonische Strukturen perfekt in Landschaft, Technologie und Innenarchitektur integriert werden.
Von Boutique-Hotels über gehobene Restaurants bis hin zu dynamischen Arbeitsräumen und Luxuswohnprojekten umfasst das in Melbourne ansässige Unternehmen eine breite Palette von Designprojekten.
Das Büro hat Anerkennung für seine Arbeit erhalten und zahlreiche Auszeichnungen wie das Balmoral Beach House gewonnen. Ihr Engagement besteht darin, außergewöhnliche architektonische Erlebnisse zu bieten, die die Erwartungen ihrer Kunden übertreffen und die Schönheit und Funktionalität jedes Raums hervorheben.

BYRNE ARCHITECTS

NICHOLAS BYRNE

byrnearchitects.com.au

Dirigé par Nicholas Byrne et une équipe créative dévouée, Byrne Architects est réputé pour ses projets où des structures emblématiques sont intégrées de manière transparente au paysage, à la technologie et à la décoration intérieure.
Des hôtels de charme aux restaurants gastronomiques, des espaces de travail dynamiques aux projets résidentiels de luxe, l'entreprise basée à Melbourne couvre un large éventail de projets de conception.
Le studio a été récompensé pour son travail et a reçu de nombreux prix pour ses projets, tels que le Balmoral Beach House. Il s'engage à offrir des expériences architecturales exceptionnelles qui dépassent les attentes de ses clients et mettent en valeur la beauté et la fonctionnalité de chaque espace.

Liderado por Nicholas Byrne y un equipo creativo especializado, Byrne Architects es reconocido por proyectos en los que las estructuras icónicas se integran perfectamente con el paisaje, la tecnología y el diseño de interiores.
Desde hoteles boutique hasta restaurantes de alta cocina, pasando por espacios de trabajo dinámicos y proyectos residenciales de lujo, la firma con sede en Melbourne abarca una amplia gama de proyectos de diseño.
El estudio ha obtenido reconocimientos por su trabajo, y ha recibido numerosos premios por sus proyectos, como el Balmoral Beach House. Su compromiso es brindar experiencias arquitectónicas excepcionales que superen las expectativas de sus clientes y resalten la belleza y funcionalidad de cada espacio.

THE WENSLEY

Wensleydale, Victoria, Australia

Photos © Sean Fennessy, Lisa Cohen

The owners hired their old friend, architect Nick Byrne, to build their family residence in a remote location on the Surf Coast of Victoria. Wensleydale is a secluded rural estate that fulfills the owners' desire for a serene retreat with vineyards, an orchard, and bathing areas.

Approaching from the road, a sequence of trees hides the view of the property. The path winds and leads to a valley carved into the terrain. The building, atop a hill, has a roof that frames the impressive views.

The interiors are elaborate and textured, with walls, floors, and ceilings constructed with different wood species and profiles. The in-situ concrete fireplace is the focal point of the space. It stands out as a sculptural element that enters into the structure. The exposed fireplace showcases a Cheminee Philippe with its iconic door rail counterweight.

The interior is warm and bright, capturing the essence of a rural home with modern design integrated into the surrounding landscape.

Die Besitzer engagierten ihren alten Freund, den Architekten Nick Byrne, um ihr Familienhaus an einem abgelegenen Ort an der Surf Coast von Victoria zu bauen. Wensleydale ist ein abgelegenes ländliches Anwesen, das dem Wunsch seiner Besitzer nach einem ruhigen Rückzugsort mit Weinbergen, einem Obstgarten und Bademöglichkeiten entspricht.

Beim Annähern von der Straße aus verbirgt eine Baumsequenz den Blick auf das Anwesen. Der Weg windet sich und führt zu einem in das Gelände eingegrabenen Tal. Das Gebäude auf einem Hügel hat ein Dach, das die atemberaubende Panoramaaussicht auf das Tal einfängt.

Die Innenräume sind aufwendig und strukturiert, mit Wänden, Böden und Decken aus verschiedenen Holzarten und Profilen. Der vor Ort gegossene Betonkamin ist der Mittelpunkt des Raums. Er ragt als skulpturales Element in die Struktur hinein. Der offene Kamin zeigt einen Cheminee Philippe mit seinem markanten Türschienengewicht.

Die Innenatmosphäre ist warm und hell und fängt die Essenz eines ländlichen Wohnhauses mit modernem Design ein, das in die umgebende Landschaft integriert ist.

Les propriétaires ont fait appel à leur ami architecte de longue date, Nick Byrne, pour construire leur résidence familiale dans un endroit isolé de la Surf Coast de Victoria. Wensleydale est un domaine isolé qui répond au désir des propriétaires d'une retraite sereine avec des vignobles, un verger et des zones de baignade.

À l'approche de la route, une succession d'arbres masque la vue sur la propriété. La route serpente et débouche sur une vallée creusée dans le sol. Le bâtiment, situé sur une colline, est coiffé d'un toit qui encadre le panorama époustouflant de la vallée.

Les intérieurs sont élaborés et texturés, avec des murs, des sols et des plafonds construits à partir de différentes essences et profils de bois. La cheminée en béton coulé sur place est le point central de l'espace. Elle s'impose comme un élément sculptural qui pénètre la structure. La cheminée exposée met en valeur une cheminée Philippe avec son emblématique contrepoids de rail de porte.

L'environnement intérieur est chaleureux et lumineux, capturant l'essence d'une habitation rurale avec un design moderne intégré dans le paysage environnant.

Los propietarios contrataron a su antiguo amigo el arquitecto, Nick Byrne, para construir su residencia familiar en un remoto paraje en la Costa del Surf de Victoria. Wensleydale es una finca rural apartada que responde al deseo de sus dueños de contar con un refugio sereno con viñedos, un huerto y zonas de baño.

Al acercarse desde la carretera, una secuencia de árboles oculta la vista de la propiedad. El camino serpentea y conduce a un valle excavado en el terreno. El edificio, en lo alto de una colina, tiene un tejado que enmarca el impresionante panorama del valle.

Los interiores son elaborados y texturizados, con paredes, suelos y techos construidos con diferentes especies y perfiles de madera. La chimenea de hormigón in situ es el punto focal del espacio. Se destaca como un elemento escultórico que penetra en la estructura. La chimenea expuesta exhibe una Cheminee Philippe con su icónico contrapeso de riel de puerta.

El ambiente interior es cálido y luminoso, capturando la esencia de una vivienda rural con un diseño moderno integrado en el paisaje circundante.

CM Natural Designs was founded in 2011 and specializes in creating designs for residential spaces. Its founder, Corine Maggio, is a renowned interior designer with extensive experience living in different regions of the United States. This geographic diversity has enriched her perspective on people's lifestyles. Thanks to this unique perspective, the company creates custom designs that reflect the individuality of each client. For Corine, a home is not simply a place to display furniture, but a space where people can feel comfortable and authentic. The Marin County, California-based studio's work has been widely appreciated and published in various trade magazines, as well as featured on HGTV.

CM Natural Designs wurde 2011 gegründet und hat sich auf die Gestaltung von Wohnräumen spezialisiert. Die Gründerin Corine Maggio ist eine renommierte Innenarchitektin mit umfangreicher Erfahrung in verschiedenen Regionen der USA. Diese geografische Vielfalt hat ihre Perspektive auf den Lebensstil der Menschen bereichert. Dank dieser einzigartigen Perspektive ist das Unternehmen in der Lage, maßgeschneiderte Designs zu schaffen, die die Individualität jedes Kunden widerspiegeln. Für Corine ist ein Zuhause nicht nur ein Ort, um Möbel auszustellen, sondern ein Raum, in dem sich Menschen wohl und authentisch fühlen können. Die Arbeit des Studios mit Sitz in Marin County, Kalifornien, wurde weitreichend anerkannt und in verschiedenen Fachzeitschriften veröffentlicht sowie auf HGTV präsentiert.

CM NATURAL DESIGNS

CORINE MAGGIO

cmnaturaldesigns.com

CM Natural Designs a été fondé en 2011 et se spécialise dans la création de designs pour les espaces résidentiels. Sa fondatrice, Corine Maggio, est une architecte d'intérieur renommée qui a vécu dans différentes régions des États-Unis. Cette diversité géographique a enrichi son regard sur les modes de vie des gens. Grâce à cette perspective unique, l'entreprise a la capacité de créer des designs personnalisés qui reflètent l'individualité de chaque client. Pour Corine, une maison n'est pas simplement un endroit où l'on expose des meubles, mais un espace où l'on se sent à l'aise et authentique. Le travail du studio basé dans le comté de Marin, en Californie, a été largement reconnu et publié dans divers magazines spécialisés, ainsi que présenté sur HGTV.

CM Natural Designs se fundó en 2011 y se especializa en la creación de diseños para espacios residenciales. Su fundadora, Corine Maggio, es una reconocida diseñadora de interiores con una amplia experiencia viviendo en diferentes regiones de Estados Unidos. Esta diversidad geográfica ha enriquecido su perspectiva sobre el estilo de vida de las personas. Gracias a esta perspectiva única, la empresa tiene la capacidad de crear diseños personalizados que reflejan la individualidad de cada cliente. Para Corine, un hogar no es simplemente un lugar para exhibir muebles, sino un espacio donde las personas puedan sentirse cómodas y auténticas. El trabajo del estudio, con sede en Marin County, California, ha sido ampliamente reconocido y publicado en diversas revistas especializadas, así como presentado en HGTV.

INVERNESS

Inverness, California, United States

Photos © Carley Page Summers

Located on the north coast of California, in a town of less than 1.500 people, this house is owned by a young couple who were looking for a retreat in nature to get away from the hustle and bustle of the city on weekends. The renovation design took advantage of the original structure designed by an architect and artist, making the necessary adjustments to improve its functionality.
Corine and her team kept the charm and character of the home but made it more practical by opening up the kitchen and creating a primary suite. Amenities such as central heating and wooden floors were also added to provide a sense of warmth both literally and figuratively. The good fortune of retaining some of the previous owner's artwork allowed her memory to be honoured in the space.
The rural setting and coastal location were influential factors in the re design, reflected in the animal imagery that evokes the surrounding farms and the use of materials related to the nautical world. The interior is dominated by neutral and light tones, avoiding distractions and allowing the stunning scenery to be enjoyed through the large windows.

Dieses Haus befindet sich an der Nordküste von Kalifornien in einer Stadt mit weniger als 1.500 Einwohnern. Es gehört einem jungen Paar, das an den Wochenenden eine Flucht in die Natur vor dem Trubel der Stadt suchte. Beim Umbau wurde die ursprüngliche Struktur, die von einem Architekten und Künstler entworfen wurde, genutzt und erforderliche Anpassungen vorgenommen, um ihre Funktionalität zu verbessern.
Die Designerin respektierte den Charme und Charakter des Hauses und machte es praktischer, indem sie die Küche öffnete und eine Hauptsuite schuf. Auch Annehmlichkeiten wie Zentralheizung und Holzböden wurden hinzugefügt, um ein Gefühl von Wärme sowohl im wörtlichen als auch im übertragenen Sinne zu vermitteln. Das Glück, einige Kunstwerke des vorherigen Eigentümers zu bewahren, ermöglichte es, seine Erinnerung im Raum zu ehren.
Die ländliche Umgebung und die Küstenlage waren prägende Faktoren für das Redesign, die sich in Bildern von Tieren widerspiegeln, die an umliegende Bauernhöfe erinnern, sowie in der Verwendung von Materialien, die mit der nautischen Welt in Verbindung stehen. Im Inneren dominieren neutrale und helle Farbtöne, um Ablenkungen zu vermeiden und den beeindruckenden Ausblick durch die großen Fenster genießen zu können.

Située sur la côte nord de la Californie, dans une ville de moins de 1 500 habitants, cette maison appartient à un jeune couple qui cherchait une retraite dans la nature pour échapper à l'agitation de la ville pendant les week-ends. Le projet de rénovation a tiré parti de la structure d'origine conçue par un architecte et un artiste, en procédant aux ajustements nécessaires pour améliorer sa fonctionnalité.
Corine et son équipe ont conservé le charme et le de la maison mais l'ont rendue plus pratique en ouvrant la cuisine et en en ouvrant la cuisine et en créant une suite principale. Des équipements tels que le chauffage central et des planchers en bois ont également été ajoutés pour apporter un sentiment de chaleur, au sens propre comme au sens figuré. La chance d'avoir conservé certaines des œuvres d'art de l'ancien propriétaire a permis d'honorer sa mémoire dans l'espace.
Le cadre rural et la situation côtière ont été des facteurs influents dans le réaménagement, comme en témoignent l'imagerie animale qui évoque les fermes environnantes et l'utilisation de matériaux liés à l'univers nautique. L'intérieur est dominé par des tons neutres et clairs, évitant les distractions et permettant d'apprécier le paysage époustouflant à travers les grandes fenêtres.

Ubicada en la costa norte de California, en un pueblo con menos de 1.500 habitantes, esta casa es propiedad de una pareja joven que buscaba un refugio en la naturaleza para alejarse los fines de semana del ajetreo en la ciudad. En el diseño de renovación, se aprovechó la estructura original diseñada por un arquitecto y artista, realizando los ajustes necesarios para mejorar su funcionalidad.
Corine y su equipo respetaron el encanto y el carácter que ya poseía la vivienda, y la hizo más práctica al abrir la cocina y crear una suite principal. También se añadieron comodidades, como la calefacción central y los suelos de madera, para brindar una sensación de calidez tanto literal como figurada. La suerte de conservar algunas de las obras de arte del propietario anterior permitió honrar su memoria en el espacio.
El entorno rural y la ubicación costera fueron factores influyentes en el rediseño, reflejados en las imágenes de animales que evocan las granjas circundantes y en el uso de materiales relacionados con el mundo náutico. En el interior predominan los tonos neutros y claros, evitando distracciones y permitiendo disfrutar del impresionante paisaje a través de los amplios ventanales.

Dalman Architects is a firm with over 20 years of experience in the field of architecture and interior design. Their focus is on creating enriching spaces that evoke positive emotions in people. With a team of 28 professionals spread across studios in Christchurch and Auckland, the firm offers its services in both New Zealand and the Asia-Pacific region.
The firm has a wide range of specialties, including urban planning, project development, architecture and interior design. Its work covers a wide range of typologies such as hotels, churches, housing, retail and urban planning. Leadership is provided by Richard Dalman, who serves as managing director and principal architect. Thanks to his experience and vision, his team has won several awards and recognitions.

Dalman Architects ist ein Büro mit über 20 Jahren Erfahrung in den Bereichen Architektur und Innenarchitektur. Der Schwerpunkt liegt auf der Schaffung von bereichernden Räumen, die bei den Menschen positive Emotionen hervorrufen. Mit einem Team von 28 Fachleuten, die sich auf Studios in Christchurch und Auckland verteilen, bietet das Büro seine Dienstleistungen sowohl in Neuseeland als auch im asiatisch-pazifischen Raum an.
Das Büro verfügt über ein breites Spektrum an Spezialgebieten, darunter Stadtplanung, Projektentwicklung, Architekturdesign und Innenarchitektur. Die Arbeit deckt ein breites Spektrum an Typologien wie Hotels, Kirchen, Wohnungen, Einzelhandel und Stadtplanung ab. Das Büro wird von Richard Dalman geleitet, der als Geschäftsführer und leitender Architekt fungiert. Dank seiner Erfahrung und seines Weitblicks hat sein Team bereits mehrere Preise und Auszeichnungen erhalten.

DALMAN ARCHITECTS

RICHARD DALMAN

dalman.co.nz

Dalman Architects est un cabinet qui compte plus de 20 ans d'expérience dans le domaine de l'architecture et de la décoration d'intérieur. Son objectif est de créer des espaces enrichissants qui suscitent des émotions positives chez les gens. Avec une équipe de 28 professionnels répartis entre les studios de Christchurch et d'Auckland, le cabinet offre ses services en Nouvelle-Zélande et dans la région Asie-Pacifique.
Le cabinet possède un large éventail de spécialités, notamment la planification urbaine, le développement de projets, la conception architecturale et l'architecture d'intérieur. Son travail couvre un large éventail de typologies telles que les hôtels, les églises, le logement, le commerce de détail et la planification urbaine. La direction est assurée par Richard Dalman, qui occupe les fonctions de directeur général et d'architecte principal. Grâce à son expérience et à sa vision, son équipe a remporté plusieurs prix et récompenses.

Dalman Architects es una firma con más de 20 años de experiencia en el campo de la arquitectura y el diseño de interiores. Su enfoque se centra en la creación de espacios enriquecedores que evocan emociones positivas en las personas. Con un equipo de 28 profesionales distribuidos en los estudios de Christchurch y Auckland, la firma ofrece sus servicios tanto en Nueva Zelanda como en la región de Asia-Pacífico.
El estudio cuenta con una amplia gama de especialidades, que incluyen planificación urbana, desarrollo de proyectos, diseño arquitectónico y diseño de interiores. Su trabajo abarca una amplia tipologías como hoteles, iglesias, viviendas, locales comerciales y planeamiento urbano. El liderazgo recae en Richard Dalman, quien ocupa el cargo de director general y arquitecto principal. Gracias a su experiencia y visión, su equipo ha obtenido varios premios y reconocimientos.

SLIDING HOUSE

Tai Tapu, New Zealand

Photos © Stephen Goodenough

This hilltop house has panoramic views of the Southern Alps, the Canterbury Plains and surrounding countryside. It comprises three separate structures, parallel to each other and connected by a central gallery space. The design intent was to create relaxed spaces in which the natural environment can be appreciated from each room. Large windows and opening screens were strategically positioned to direct views in various directions.

A skylight over the kitchen offers an interesting play of light while the tones of the surrounding landscape are reflected on the white walls. The master bedroom overlooks a wooded ravine – a tranquil setting for relaxation.

The outdoor spaces are adapted to the climatic conditions. A walled courtyard divides the main house from the guest area, creating a protected garden. Natural materials such as cedar enhance the beauty of the residence and acquire a grayish patina over time. This home delivers a calm tranquility and optimises the stunning landscape vistas for its residents.

Dieses Haus auf dem Hügel bietet einen Panoramablick auf die Südalpen, die Canterbury-Ebene und die umliegende Landschaft. Es besteht aus drei separaten Strukturen, die parallel zueinander angeordnet sind und durch einen zentralen Galerieraum miteinander verbunden sind. Die Designintention war es, entspannte Räume zu schaffen, in denen die natürliche Umgebung von jedem Zimmer aus genossen werden kann. Große Fenster und öffnende Bildschirme wurden strategisch platziert, um den Blick in verschiedene Richtungen zu lenken.

Ein Oberlicht über der Küche bietet ein interessantes Spiel mit Licht, während die Farbtöne der umliegenden Landschaft an den weißen Wänden reflektiert werden. Das Hauptschlafzimmer blickt auf eine bewaldete Schlucht - eine ruhige Umgebung zur Entspannung.

Die Außenbereiche sind an die klimatischen Bedingungen angepasst. Ein ummauerter Innenhof trennt das Hauptgebäude vom Gästebereich und schafft einen geschützten Garten. Natürliche Materialien wie Zeder erhöhen die Schönheit der Residenz und entwickeln im Laufe der Zeit eine grau-braune Patina. Dieses Zuhause strahlt eine ruhige Gelassenheit aus und optimiert die atemberaubende Landschaft für seine Bewohner.

Située au sommet d'une colline, cette maison offre une vue panoramique sur les Alpes du Sud, les plaines de Canterbury et la campagne environnante. Elle se compose de trois structures distinctes, parallèles les unes aux autres et reliées par une galerie centrale. L'objectif de la conception était de créer des espaces détendus permettant d'apprécier l'environnement naturel depuis chaque pièce. À cette fin, de grandes fenêtres et des écrans ont été stratégiquement placés pour orienter les vues dans différentes directions.

Le puits de lumière au-dessus de la cuisine offre un jeu de lumière intéressant, tandis que les tons du paysage environnant se reflètent dans les murs blancs. La chambre principale donne sur un ravin boisé, un cadre paisible propice à la détente.

Les espaces extérieurs sont adaptés aux conditions climatiques. Une cour entourée de murs sépare la maison principale de la zone des invités, créant ainsi un jardin abrité. Les matériaux naturels tels que le cèdre rehaussent la beauté de la résidence et acquièrent une patine grisâtre au fil du temps. La maison transmet une tranquillité sereine et optimise les vues à couper le souffle sur le paysage pour ses résidents.

Situada en lo alto de una colina, esta casa ofrece vistas panorámicas de los Alpes del Sur, las llanuras de Canterbury y la campiña circundante. Consta de tres estructuras independientes, paralelas entre sí y conectadas por una galería central. La intención del diseño ha sido crear espacios distendidos para apreciar el entorno natural desde cada habitación. Para ello, se colocaron estratégicamente grandes ventanales y mamparas que dirigen las vistas en varias direcciones.

La claraboya sobre la cocina ofrece un interesante juego de luces, mientras que los tonos del paisaje circundante se reflejan en las paredes blancas. El dormitorio principal tiene vistas a un barranco boscoso, un entorno tranquilo para relajarse.

Los espacios exteriores están adaptados a las condiciones climáticas. Un patio amurallado divide la casa principal de la zona de invitados, creando un jardín protegido. Materiales naturales como el cedro realzan la belleza de la residencia y adquieren una pátina grisácea con el paso del tiempo. La casa transmite una serena tranquilidad y optimiza las impresionantes vistas del paisaje para sus residentes.

Floor plan

1. Deck
2. Entry
3. Laundry
4. Study
5. Garage
6. Service court
7. Gallery
8. Bedroom
9. Bathroom
10. Hall
11. Ensuite
12. Master bedroom
13. Kitchen garden
14. Toilet
15. Pantry
16. Lounge
17. Kitchen
18. Dining
19. Living
20. Courtyard
21. Path
22. Guest wing bedroom
23. Linen

ELLIOTT ARCHITECTS

Elliott Architects approach design with a consistent philosophy, focusing on creating meaningful buildings which meet the needs of their users with attention to detail and sensitivity to context.
Founded by Ben and Lynsey Elliott in 2014, the Northumberland based practice have developed a reputation for design focused architecture and close client relationships. Often working on cultural and residential projects, their subtle designs create contemporary architecture in sensitive historic and rural contexts.
Their quiet yet sophisticated approach to design has led to multiple prestigious architecture awards including four regional RIBA Awards, an RIBA Conservation Award, three RIBA "Small Project of the Year Awards" as well as a coveted RIBA National Award in 2023.

Elliott Architects verfolgen bei der Gestaltung eine konsequente Philosophie und konzentrieren sich darauf, sinnvolle Gebäude zu schaffen, die die Bedürfnisse ihrer Nutzer mit funktionalen Lösungen, Liebe zum Detail und Sensibilität für den Kontext erfüllen.
Das 2014 von Ben und Lynsey Elliott gegründete Büro mit Sitz in Northumberland hat sich einen Ruf für designorientierte Architektur und enge Kundenbeziehungen erworben. Ihre subtilen Entwürfe, mit denen sie häufig an Kultur- und Wohnprojekten arbeiten, schaffen zeitgenössische Architektur in sensiblen historischen und ländlichen Kontexten.
Ihr ruhiger und doch anspruchsvoller Ansatz hat zu zahlreichen renommierten Architekturpreisen geführt, darunter neun vier regionale RIBA Awards, darunter ein RIBA Conservation Award, und drei „RIBA Small Project of the Year Awards" sowie ein begehrter RIBA National Award im Jahr 2023.

ELLIOTT ARCHITECTS

BEN ELLIOTT, LYNSEY ELLIOTT

elliottarchitects.co.uk

Elliott Architects aborde la conception avec une philosophie cohérente, en se concentrant sur la création de bâtiments significatifs qui répondent aux besoins des utilisateurs avec des solutions fonctionnelles, une attention aux détails et une sensibilité au contexte.
Fondé par Ben et Lynsey Elliott en 2014, le cabinet basé dans le Northumberland s'est forgé une réputation pour son architecture axée sur le design et ses relations étroites avec ses clients. Il travaille souvent sur des projets culturels et résidentiels et ses projets visent une architecture contemporaine dans des contextes historiques et ruraux.
Son souci du détail et son approche à la fois simple et sophistiquée de la conception lui ont valu un certain nombre de récompenses architecturales, notamment quatre prix régionaux du RIBA, un prix de la conservation du RIBA, trois prix « Small Project of the Year Awards » du RIBA, ainsi qu'un très convoité prix national du RIBA en 2023.

El estudio Elliott Architects aborda el diseño con una filosofía coherente, centrándose en la creación de edificios significativos que satisfacen las necesidades de los usuarios con soluciones funcionales, atención al detalle y sensibilidad al contexto.
Fundado por Ben y Lynsey Elliott en 2014, este estudio con sede en Northumberland se ha labrado una reputación en base a su arquitectura centrada en el diseño y las estrechas relaciones con los clientes. Trabaja a menudo en proyectos culturales y residenciales y sus proyectos apuntan a una arquitectura contemporánea en contextos históricos y rurales.
Su atención al detalle y su enfoque simple pero sofisticado del diseño, le ha valido varios premios de arquitectura, incluidos cuatro premios regionales RIBA, un premio RIBA de Conservación, tres premios RIBA al «Small Project of the Year Award», así como un codiciado Premio Nacional RIBA en 2023.

NORTH BANK

Tyne Valley, Northumberland, United Kingdom

Photos © Jill Tate

This house sits on the hillside above the Tyne valley, orientating its form in relation to the panoramic views towards the Pennine hills. The setting required a sensitive approach, and so the design reinterprets elements of Northumberland's historic agricultural buildings, many of which were heather thatched with steeply pitched roofs. The elegant proportions are utilised internally to create a dramatic space which is lofty, but with a softness reminiscent of a humble rural chapel. Context was a key consideration, and the design draws the eye to the wonderful views whilst maintaining privacy with its neighbours. Internally views are carefully framed rather than expansive, offering a feeling of protection and privacy. The mining of metals was once the key industry of the area, and this historic connection influenced the use of zinc for the roof, used in its natural, unfinished state. The materials create a lightness to the design, and when seen from the south, the distinctive gable floats in the trees as the ground sharply falls away. Although different to its neighbours, the design is rooted in the local physical and historic context and has been sensitively designed to embody the spirit of its place.

Das Haus liegt an einem Hang oberhalb des Tyne-Tals und orientiert sich in seiner Form an den Panorama-blicken auf die Pennine-Hügel. Die Umgebung erforderte einen sensiblen Ansatz, und so interpretiert der Entwurf Elemente der historischen landwirtschaftlichen Gebäude Northumberlands neu, von denen viele mit Heidekraut gedeckt waren und steile Dächer hatten. Die eleganten Proportionen werden im Inneren genutzt, um einen dramatischen Raum zu schaffen, der erhaben ist, aber mit einer Sanftheit, die an eine bescheidene ländliche Kapelle erinnert. Der Kontext war eine wichtige Überlegung, und der Entwurf lenkt den Blick auf die wunderbare Aussicht, ohne die Privatsphäre der Nachbarn zu beeinträchtigen. Die Innen-räume sind sorgfältig umrahmt und bieten ein Gefühl von Schutz und Privatsphäre. Der Metallabbau war einst die Schlüsselindustrie der Gegend, und diese historische Verbindung beeinflusste die Verwendung von Zink für das Dach, das in seinem natürlichen, unbearbeiteten Zustand verwendet wurde. Das Material verleiht dem Entwurf eine gewisse Leichtigkeit, und von Süden aus gesehen schwebt der markante Giebel in den Bäumen, während der Boden steil abfällt. Obwohl es sich von seinen Nachbarn unterscheidet, ist der Entwurf in den örtlichen und historischen Gegebenheiten verwurzelt und wurde sensibel gestaltet, um den Geist des Ortes zu verkörpern.

Cette maison, située sur les pentes de la vallée de la Tyne, est orientée en fonction des vues panoramiques sur les collines de la Pennine. Le cadre exigeant une approche sensible, la conception réinterprète les bâ-timents agricoles historiques du Northumberland, avec leurs toits de chaume et leurs pentes prononcées. Les proportions élégantes sont exploitées à l'intérieur pour créer un espace spectaculaire, surélevé mais avec une délicatesse qui rappelle une modeste chapelle de campagne. Le contexte était un élément clé, et la conception attire l'attention sur les vues magnifiques tout en préservant l'intimité avec les voisins. À l'intérieur, les vues sont encadrées plutôt qu'étendues, offrant un sentiment de protection et d'intimité. L'extraction de métaux était autrefois l'industrie clé de la région, et ce lien historique a influencé l'utilisa-tion du zinc pour le toit, utilisé dans son état naturel et non fini. Les matériaux ajoutent de la légèreté à la conception et, vu du sud, le pignon distinctif flotte parmi les arbres à mesure que le terrain recule. Bien que différent de ses voisins, le projet est ancré dans le contexte physique et historique local et a été conçu avec sensibilité pour incarner cet esprit.

Esta casa que se asienta en la ladera del valle del Tyne, está orientada a las vistas panorámicas de las colinas de los Peninos. El entorno exigía un planteamiento sensible, por lo que el diseño reinterpreta los edificios agrícolas históricos de Northumberland, con tejados de paja y pendientes pronunciadas. Las ele-gantes proporciones se aprovechan en el interior para crear un espacio espectacular, elevado pero con una delicadeza que recuerda a una humilde capilla rural. El contexto fue una consideración clave, y el diseño atrae la mirada hacia las maravillosas vistas al tiempo que mantiene la privacidad con sus vecinos. En el interior, las vistas están enmarcadas en lugar de ser expansivas, lo que ofrece una sensación de protección e intimidad. La minería de metales fue en su día la industria clave de la zona, y esta conexión histórica influyó en el uso del zinc para el tejado, utilizado en su estado natural e inacabado. Los materiales apor-tan ligereza al diseño y, visto desde el sur, el característico frontón flota entre los árboles a medida que el terreno se aleja. Aunque diferente de sus vecinos, el diseño está enraizado en el contexto físico e histórico local y se ha concebido con sensibilidad para encarnar ese espíritu.

Fernando Fernández, who has led Estudio FES since 2015, has focused his career on residential, commercial and equipment projects, always demonstrating his concern for aesthetics and details.
Alfredo Edwards, founder of EV Arquitectos, has also dedicated his career to residential and urban design, complemented by industrial and territorial planning. The emphasis is on spatial, functional and constructive aspects.
The work of both architects, graduates of the Pontificia Universidad Católica de Chile, provided an integral solution to the brief and the different scales of the projects, offering functional and sustainable solutions for the local context.
The Zaguán House, developed jointly by the two studios based in Santiago de Chile, is one of the collaborative projects that have managed to leave their mark on the local architectural landscape.

Fernando Fernández, der Estudio FES seit 2015 leitet, hat sich in seiner Laufbahn auf Wohn-, Gewerbe- und Ausstattungsprojekte konzentriert und dabei stets sein Interesse für Ästhetik und Details bewiesen.
Alfredo Edwards, Gründer von EV Arquitectos, hat seine Karriere ebenfalls dem Wohn- und Städtebau gewidmet, ergänzt durch Industrie- und Raumplanung. Der Schwerpunkt liegt dabei auf räumlichen, funktionalen und konstruktiven Aspekten.
Die Arbeit der beiden Architekten, die Absolventen der Pontificia Universidad Católica de Chile sind, bot eine ganzheitliche Lösung für die Aufgabenstellung und die verschiedenen Maßstäbe der Projekte, die funktionale und nachhaltige Lösungen für den lokalen Kontext bieten.
Das Haus Zaguán, das von den beiden in Santiago de Chile ansässigen Büros gemeinsam entwickelt wurde, ist eines der gemeinsamen Projekte, die der lokalen Architekturlandschaft ihren Stempel aufgedrückt haben.

ESTUDIO FES, EV ARQUITECTOS

FERNANDO FERNÁNDEZ, ALFREDO EDWARDS

estudiofes.cl

Fernando Fernández, qui dirige Estudio FES depuis 2015, a axé sa carrière sur des projets résidentiels, commerciaux et d'équipement, en mettant toujours l'accent sur son souci de l'esthétique et des détails.
Alfredo Edwards, fondateur d'EV Arquitectos, a également consacré sa carrière à la conception résidentielle et urbaine, complétée par la planification industrielle et territoriale. Il met l'accent sur les aspects spatiaux, fonctionnels et constructifs.
Le travail des deux architectes, diplômés de la Pontificia Universidad Católica de Chile, a permis d'apporter une solution intégrale à la commande et aux différentes échelles du projet, en fournissant des solutions fonctionnelles et durables pour le contexte local.
La maison Zaguán, développée en collaboration par les deux studios basés à Santiago du Chili, est l'un des projets sur lesquels ils ont travaillé ensemble et qui ont réussi à laisser leur marque dans le paysage architectural local.

Fernando Fernández, quien dirige Estudio FES desde el año 2015, ha enfocado su carrera en proyectos residenciales, comerciales y de equipamiento, siempre destacando su preocupación por lo estético y por los detalles.
Alfredo Edwards, fundador de EV Arquitectos, ha dedicado también su carrera al diseño residencial y urbano, complementado con la planificación industrial y territorial. Poniendo énfasis en aspectos espaciales, funcionales y constructivos.
El trabajo de ambos arquitectos, egresados de la Pontificia Universidad Católica de Chile, dio una solución integral al encargo y a las distintas escalas de proyecto, entregando soluciones funcionales y sostenibles para el contexto local.
La Casa Zaguán desarrollada colaborativamente por ambos estudios con sede en Santiago de Chile, es uno de los proyectos trabajados en conjunto que han logrado dejar su huella en el paisaje arquitectónico local.

CASA ZAGUÁN

Lago Colico, Namoncahue, X Región, Chile

Photos © Fernando Fernández, José Tomás Schmidt

Located on an elevation overlooking the landscape, this house comprises two dwellings in a single structure: one for a resident family and one for visitors. Both units have a single roof and are connected by a translucent roof space that serves as an entrance hall. One of the units faces north and the other south, so that each house has an individual relationship to its surroundings. This position ensures adequate lighting and ventilation to cope with seasonal climatic changes.
The simple layout and the height of the roof allows for the creation of volumes that control climatic variations and, at the same time, generate ample space for common areas. Inside each unit, there is a central double-height space around which the private rooms are distributed, encouraging sociability. The cladding is made of cypress pine. The roof and the south wall are protected with zinc sheets to cope with the increased exposure to humidity. In addition, the interior of the house is covered with *Radiata* pine bleached with diluted paint, which improves the lighting and preserves the warmth of the wood.

Dieses Haus befindet sich auf einer Anhöhe mit Blick auf die Landschaft und besteht aus zwei Wohnungen in einer einzigen Struktur: eine für eine dort lebende Familie und eine für Besucher. Beide Einheiten haben ein einzigartiges Dach und sind durch einen Raum mit transluzidem Dach verbunden, der als Eingangsbereich dient. Eine der Einheiten ist nach Norden und die andere nach Süden ausgerichtet, so dass jedes Haus eine individuelle Beziehung zur Umgebung hat. Diese Position gewährleistet eine angemessene Beleuchtung und Belüftung, um auf die saisonalen Wetterveränderungen reagieren zu können.
Die einfache Anordnung und die Höhe des Dachs ermöglichen die Schaffung von Volumina, die klimatische Variationen kontrollieren und gleichzeitig großzügige Gemeinschaftsbereiche schaffen. Im Inneren jeder Einheit befindet sich ein zentraler zweigeschossiger Raum, um den herum die privaten Zimmer angeordnet sind, um das Zusammenleben zu fördern. Die Verkleidung besteht aus Zypressenholz. Das Dach und die südliche Wand sind mit Zinkplatten geschützt, um der erhöhten Feuchtigkeit standzuhalten. Darüber hinaus ist das Innere des Hauses mit aufgehelltem *Radiata*-Kiefernholz überzogen, was die Beleuchtung verbessert und die Wärme des Holzes bewahrt.

Située sur une élévation surplombant le paysage, cette maison comprend deux habitations dans une seule structure : une pour une famille résidente et une pour les visiteurs. Les deux unités ont un toit unique et sont reliées par un espace de toit translucide qui sert de hall d'entrée. L'une des unités est orientée vers le nord et l'autre vers le sud, de sorte que chaque maison a une relation individuelle avec son environnement. Cette position garantit un éclairage et une ventilation adéquats pour faire face aux changements climatiques saisonniers.
La simplicité du plan et la hauteur du toit permettent de créer des volumes qui contrôlent les variations climatiques et, en même temps, génèrent un vaste espace pour les parties communes. À l'intérieur de chaque unité, il y a un espace central à double hauteur autour duquel les chambres privées sont distribuées, ce qui favorise la convivialité. Le bardage est en pin cyprès. Le toit et le mur sud sont protégés par des feuilles de zinc pour faire face à l'exposition accrue à l'humidité. Par ailleurs, l'intérieur de la maison est recouvert de pin *radiata* blanchi à la peinture diluée, ce qui améliore l'éclairage et préserve la chaleur du bois.

Ubicado en una elevación con vistas al paisaje, esta casa comprende dos viviendas en una única estructura: una para una familia residente y otra para visitantes. Ambas unidades tienen una cubierta única y están conectadas por un espacio con techo traslúcido que sirve como zaguán de acceso. Una de las unidades se orienta al norte y la otra al sur, por lo que cada casa tiene una relación individual con el entorno. Esta posición garantiza una adecuada iluminación y ventilación para enfrentar los cambios climáticos estacionales.
La disposición sencilla y la altura de la cubierta permite crear volúmenes que controlan las variaciones climáticas y, al mismo tiempo, generan amplios espacios para áreas comunes. En el interior de cada unidad, se encuentra un espacio central de doble altura alrededor del cual se distribuyen las habitaciones privadas, fomentando la convivencia. El revestimiento es madera de pino ciprés. El tejado y el muro sur están protegidos con planchas de zinc para enfrentar la mayor exposición a la humedad. Además, el interior de la vivienda está recubierto con pino *radiata* blanqueado con pintura diluida, que mejora la iluminación y conserva la calidez de la madera.

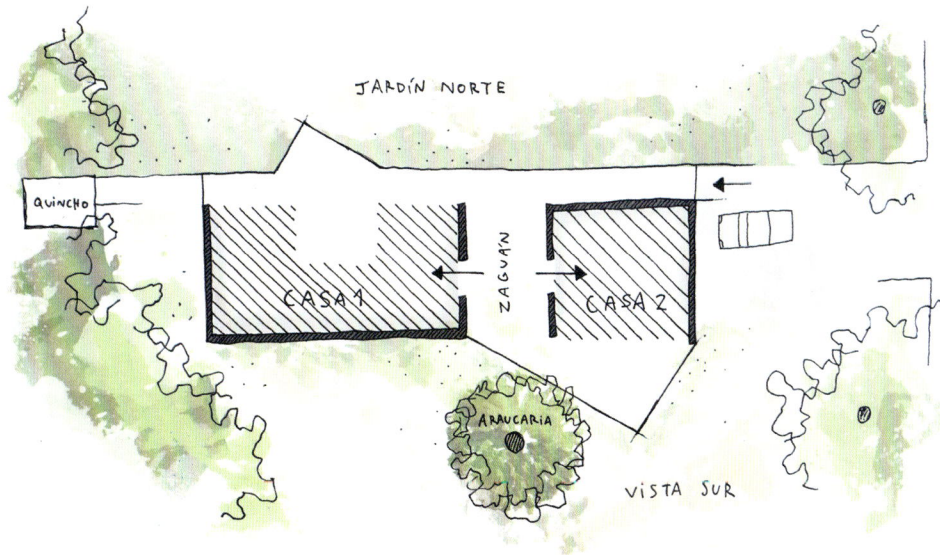

Sketch site plan

Led by father and son, Stan and Jess Field, the firm is known for practicing architecture that is deeply connected to its surroundings. Their work is like a series of moments that embrace the subtleties of place and engage with the environment. With two generations of experience in creating spaces, Field architects have created a process called "groundscape." From this point of view, each space is approached by revealing its identity through form, material, space and light. Each site is considered on its own merits, whether it be stunning ocean view or vineyards rooted in cultural history. Field values the passage of wildlife, seasonal winds and the beauty of nature. For them, a space is more than just a property, it is a sanctuary.

Das von Vater und Sohn, Stan und Jess Field, geführte Büro ist bekannt für seine Architektur, die eng mit der Umgebung verbunden ist. Ihre Arbeit ist eine Reihe von Momenten, die die Feinheiten des Ortes aufgreifen und sich mit der Umgebung auseinandersetzen. Mit der Erfahrung von zwei Generationen in der Gestaltung von Räumen haben die Architekten von Field einen Prozess entwickelt, der „groundscape" genannt wird. Von diesem Standpunkt aus wird jeder Raum betrachtet, indem seine Identität durch Form, Material, Raum und Licht enthüllt wird. Jeder Ort wird für sich betrachtet, ob es sich nun um einen atemberaubenden Blick auf den Ozean oder um kulturgeschichtlich verwurzelte Weinberge handelt. Field schätzt den Durchgang von Wildtieren, saisonale Winde und die Schönheit der Natur. Für sie ist ein Raum mehr als nur ein Grundstück, er ist ein Zufluchtsort.

FIELD ARCHITECTURE

STAN FIELD, JESS FIELD

fieldarchitecture.com

Dirigé par le père et le fils, Stan et Jess Field, le cabinet est connu pour sa pratique d'une architecture profondément liée à son environnement. Leur travail est une série de moments qui embrassent les subtilités du lieu et s'engagent avec l'environnement. Avec deux générations d'expérience dans la création d'espaces, les architectes de Field ont créé un processus appelé « groundscape ». De ce point de vue, chaque espace est abordé en révélant son identité à travers la forme, le matériau, l'espace et la lumière. Chaque site est considéré selon ses propres mérites, qu'il s'agisse d'une vue imprenable sur l'océan ou de vignobles enracinés dans l'histoire culturelle. Field apprécie le passage de la faune, les vents saisonniers et la beauté de la nature. Pour eux, un espace est plus qu'une simple propriété, c'est un sanctuaire.

Dirigida por padre e hijo, Stan y Jess Field, la firma se caracteriza por practicar una arquitectura profundamente conectada con su entorno. Su obra es como una serie de momentos que abrazan las sutilezas del lugar y se involucran con el medio ambiente. Con dos generaciones de experiencia en la creación de espacios, los arquitectos de Field han creado un proceso llamado «groundscape». Desde este punto de vista la aproximación a cada espacio se realiza revelando su identidad a través de la forma, el material, el espacio y la luz. Cada sitio es considerado a partir de sus propios méritos, ya sea unas impresionantes vistas al océano o unos viñedos arraigados en la historia cultural. Field valora el paso de la vida silvestre, los vientos estacionales y la belleza de la naturaleza. Para ellos, un espacio es más que una simple propiedad, es un santuario.

DAWNRIDGE

Los Altos Hills, California, United States

Photos © Joe Fletcher

Located in the suburban environment of Silicon Valley, this house sits on a reclaimed fragment of nature. The project is a model of responsive development, where architecture and ecological health depend on each other. Thus, more than 50 percent of the site was dedicated to habitat with the restoration of a seasonal stream and the preservation of trees, including a magnificent blue oak. The house is shaped like a traditional American ranch with little slope and bifurcates around the large oak tree to create a courtyard. The northern half diverges to follow the curve of the creek. The residence radiates elegant simplicity and layers of transparency. Materials reflect the colors and textures of the region through a minimalist palette. Concrete floors with high fly ash content, glass walls and sliding doors, and reclaimed cypress furniture contribute to the aesthetic. The exterior siding is Alaskan yellow cedar laid in thin vertical slats, a contemporary interpretation of traditional board-and-batten siding. Over time, the materials weather gracefully, revealing their nature and blending in with the beauty of the site.

Dieses Haus in der Vorstadt von Silicon Valley steht auf einem zurückgewonnenen Stückchen Natur. Das Projekt ist ein Modell für eine verantwortungsbewusste Entwicklung, bei der Architektur und ökologische Gesundheit voneinander abhängen. So wurden mehr als 50 % des Grundstücks dem Lebensraum gewidmet, indem ein jahreszeitlich bedingter Bachlauf wiederhergestellt und Bäume, darunter eine prächtige blaue Eiche, erhalten wurden. Das Haus hat die Form einer traditionellen amerikanischen Ranch mit sanftem Gefälle und gliedert sich um die große Eiche herum, um einen Innenhof zu schaffen. Die nördliche Hälfte weicht ab und folgt dem Verlauf des Baches. Das Haus strahlt eine elegante Einfachheit und Transparenz aus. Die Materialien spiegeln die Farben und Texturen der Region in einer minimalistischen Farbpalette wider. Betonböden mit hohem Flugascheanteil, Glaswände und Glasschiebetüren sowie Möbel aus recycelten Zypressen tragen zur Ästhetik bei. Die Außenverkleidung besteht aus gelber Zeder aus Alaska, die in dünnen vertikalen Latten verlegt ist, eine moderne Interpretation der traditionellen Bretterverschalung mit Lattung. Im Laufe der Zeit verwittern die Materialien anmutig, offenbaren ihre Natur und fügen sich in die Schönheit des Ortes ein.

Située dans la banlieue de la Silicon Valley, cette maison se trouve sur un fragment de nature récupéré. Le projet est un modèle de développement réactif, où l'architecture et la santé écologique dépendent l'une de l'autre. Ainsi, plus de 50 % du site a été consacré à l'habitat avec la restauration d'un ruisseau saisonnier et la préservation des arbres, dont un magnifique chêne bleu. La maison a la forme d'un ranch américain traditionnel avec une pente douce et se divise autour du grand chêne pour créer une cour. La moitié nord s'écarte pour suivre la courbe du ruisseau. La résidence rayonne d'une élégante simplicité et de couches de transparence. Les matériaux reflètent les couleurs et les textures de la région à travers une palette minimaliste. Les sols en béton à forte teneur en cendres volantes, les murs et les portes coulissantes en verre, ainsi que les meubles en cyprès récupérés contribuent à l'esthétique. Le bardage extérieur est en cèdre jaune d'Alaska posé en fines lamelles verticales, une interprétation contemporaine du bardage traditionnel en planches et lattes. Au fil du temps, les matériaux s'altèrent gracieusement, révélant leur nature et se fondant dans la beauté du site.

Situada en el entorno suburbano de Silicon Valley, esta casa se asienta en un fragmento recuperado de naturaleza. El proyecto es un modelo de desarrollo receptivo, donde la arquitectura y la salud ecológica dependen la una de la otra. Así, más del 50 por ciento del terreno se dedicó al hábitat con la restauración de un arroyo estacional y la conservación de los árboles, incluido un magnífico roble azul. La casa tiene la forma de un rancho tradicional americano con escasa pendiente y se bifurca en torno al gran roble para crear un patio. La mitad norte se desvía para seguir la curva del arroyo. La residencia irradia una elegante sencillez y diferentes capas de transparencia. Los materiales reflejan los colores y texturas de la región a través de una paleta minimalista. Suelos de hormigón con alto contenido de ceniza volante, paredes y puertas correderas de cristal y muebles de ciprés recuperado, contribuyen a la estética. El revestimiento exterior es de cedro amarillo de Alaska dispuesto en finas lamas verticales, una interpretación contemporánea del revestimiento tradicional de tablas y listones. Con el paso del tiempo, los materiales se desgastan con elegancia, revelando su naturaleza y mezclándose con la belleza del lugar.

Antony Mattiuzzo and Valentina Cendron founded Hoto Studio in 2013, after having collaborated individually with other architectural firms. The studio focusses in architectural design, renovations and interior design, focusing mainly on building restoration. Its work is based on understanding the architectural typologies and construction criteria of historic-agrarian buildings, while exploring new forms of contemporary living to create innovative design practices.

The studio's primary goal is to help clients create customized living spaces that suit their needs and lifestyles. Attention to detail is a fundamental element of the design and is embodied through a constant presence on site and the analytical development of every construction detail.

Antony Mattiuzzo und Valentina Cendron gründeten Hoto Studio im Jahr 2013, nachdem sie zuvor individuell mit anderen Architekturbüros zusammengearbeitet hatten. Das Studio ist auf architektonisches Design, Renovierungen und Innenraumgestaltung spezialisiert und konzentriert sich hauptsächlich auf die Restaurierung von Gebäuden. Ihre Arbeit basiert auf dem Verständnis architektonischer Typologien und konstruktiver Kriterien historisch-agrarischer Gebäude und erkundet gleichzeitig neue Formen zeitgenössischen Lebens, um innovative Designpraktiken zu schaffen.

Das Hauptziel des Studios ist es, Kunden dabei zu helfen, maßgeschneiderte Wohnräume zu schaffen, die ihren Bedürfnissen und Lebensstilen entsprechen. Die Liebe zum Detail ist ein wesentliches Element des Designs und wird durch eine ständige Präsenz auf der Baustelle und die analytische Entwicklung jedes konstruktiven Details verwirklicht.

HOTO STUDIO

ANTONY MATTIUZZO, VALENTINA CENDRON

hotostudio.it

Antony Mattiuzzo et Valentina Cendron ont fondé Hoto Studio en 2013, après avoir collaboré individuellement avec d'autres cabinets d'architectes. Le studio est spécialisé dans la conception architecturale, les rénovations et le design d'intérieur, en se concentrant principalement sur la restauration de bâtiments. Son travail est basé sur la compréhension des typologies architecturales et des critères de construction des bâtiments historico-agricoles, tout en explorant de nouvelles formes de vie contemporaine pour créer des pratiques de conception innovantes.

L'objectif principal du studio est d'aider les clients à créer des espaces de vie personnalisés qui répondent à leurs besoins et à leur mode de vie. Le souci du détail est un élément fondamental de la conception et se traduit par une présence constante sur le terrain et par le développement analytique de chaque détail de la construction.

Antony Mattiuzzo y Valentina Cendron fundaron Hoto Studio en el 2013, tras haber colaborado en forma individual con otros despachos de arquitectura. El estudio se especializa en diseño arquitectónico, renovaciones y diseño de interiores, enfocándose principalmente en la restauración de edificios. Su trabajo se basa en la comprensión de las tipologías arquitectónicas y los criterios constructivos de edificaciones histórico-agrarias, a la vez que explora nuevas formas de vida contemporáneas para crear prácticas de diseño innovadoras.

El objetivo principal del estudio es ayudar a los clientes a crear espacios de vida personalizados que se adapten a sus necesidades y estilos de vida. La atención al detalle es un elemento fundamental del diseño y se materializa mediante una presencia constante en la obra y el desarrollo analítico de cada detalle constructivo.

ZETA HOUSES (CASA YZ – CASA AS)

Jesolo, Venezia, Italy

Photos © Alessandro Lana

The "Zeta Houses" are two single-family dwellings built in an agricultural area of Venice. Although sisters, the houses are not identical, as they were designed with the same concept in mind, but adapted to the needs of each family. The architects studied the surroundings and referred to the model of the nearby farmhouses, when this marshy area was transformed into arable and inhabited land. The design borrows concepts from the "constructive intelligence" of the local ancestors. That is: compact and simple volumes; coherent orientation to sun, wind and humidity; gabled roofs; and integrated porches to take advantage of light in winter and shade in summer. In addition, the houses are on the margins of the plots so as not to waste agricultural land.
The interior layout was designed from the inside out with proportion and balance in mind, resulting in dynamic environments and fluid transitional spaces. Windows frame the views. Special attention was given to lighting, which varies throughout the day and the seasons, enhancing the sense of spatial continuity.

Die „Zeta-Häuser" sind zwei Einfamilienhäuser, die in einer landwirtschaftlichen Gegend von Venedig errichtet wurden. Obwohl sie sich ähneln, sind die Häuser nicht identisch, da sie unter Berücksichtigung des gleichen Konzepts entworfen wurden, aber den Bedürfnissen jeder Familie angepasst sind. Die Architekten haben die Umgebung studiert und sich am Modell der landwirtschaftlichen Häuser in der Umgebung orientiert, als dieses sumpfige Gebiet in bebaute und bewohnbare Flächen umgewandelt wurde. Das Design schöpft aus dem „intelligenten Konstruktionswissen" der lokalen Vorfahren. Das bedeutet kompakte und einfache Volumina, eine konsequente Ausrichtung zur Sonne, den Winden und der Feuchtigkeit, Satteldächer und integrierte Veranden, um das Licht im Winter zu nutzen und im Sommer Schatten zu spenden. Darüber hinaus befinden sich die Häuser am Rand der Parzellen, um landwirtschaftliche Flächen nicht zu verschwenden.
Die Innenraumgestaltung wurde von innen nach außen konzipiert und berücksichtigt Proportionen und Ausgewogenheit, was zu dynamischen Räumen und fließenden Übergängen führt. Die Fenster rahmen die Ausblicke ein. Besondere Aufmerksamkeit wurde der Beleuchtung gewidmet, die sich im Laufe des Tages und der Jahreszeiten ändert und so das Gefühl von räumlicher Kontinuität verstärkt.

Les « maisons Zeta » sont deux habitations unifamiliales construites dans une zone agricole de Venise. Bien que sœurs, les maisons ne sont pas identiques, car elles ont été conçues selon le même concept, mais adaptées aux besoins de chaque famille. Les architectes ont étudié les environs et se sont référés au modèle des fermes environnantes, lorsque cette zone marécageuse a été transformée en terre arable et habitée. La conception emprunte des concepts à « l'intelligence constructive » des ancêtres locaux. Il s'agit de volumes compacts et simples, d'une orientation cohérente par rapport au soleil, au vent et à l'humidité, de toits à pignons et de porches intégrés pour profiter de la lumière en hiver et de l'ombre en été. En outre, les maisons sont situées en marge des parcelles afin de ne pas gaspiller de terres agricoles.
L'aménagement intérieur a été conçu de l'intérieur vers l'extérieur en tenant compte des proportions et de l'équilibre, ce qui permet de créer des environnements dynamiques et des espaces de transition fluides. Les fenêtres encadrent les vues. Une attention particulière a été accordée à l'éclairage, qui varie au cours de la journée et des saisons, renforçant ainsi le sentiment de continuité spatiale.

Las «Zeta Houses» son dos viviendas unifamiliares construidas en una zona agrícola de Venecia. Aunque hermanas, las casas no son idénticas, ya que se diseñaron teniendo en cuenta el mismo concepto, pero adaptándose a las necesidades de cada familia. Los arquitectos estudiaron el entorno y se remitieron al modelo de las casas agrícolas del entorno, cuando esta zona pantanosa se transformó en terrenos cultivables y habitados. El diseño toma prestados conceptos de la «inteligencia constructiva» de los antepasados locales. Esto es: volúmenes compactos y simples; orientación coherente al sol, los vientos y la humedad; tejados a dos aguas, y porches integrados para aprovechar la luz en invierno y dar sombra en verano. Además, las casas están en los márgenes de las parcelas para no desperdiciar terreno agrícola.
La distribución interior se diseñó de adentro hacia afuera considerando la proporción y el equilibrio, lo que resultó en ambientes dinámicos y espacios de transición fluidos. Las ventanas enmarcan las vistas. Se dedicó una atención especial a la iluminación, la cual varía a lo largo del día y las estaciones, realzando así la sensación de continuidad espacial.

This architecture and interior design studio has its offices in the heart of Detroit, Michigan. It was founded in 2018 by David Iannuzzi, a graduate of the Taubman School of Architecture at the University of Michigan, and focuses on design at a variety of scales, including housing, restaurants, civic, art, and commercial spaces.

The firm works in different styles, backed by extensive research and knowledge of craftsmanship, construction, and materials, resulting in subtle, elegant, and innovative designs for which it is renowned. With a deep curiosity for the lifestyles and needs of its clients, Iannuzzi Studio designs comfortable spaces that can only be enriched by being lived in.

Dieses Architektur- und Innenarchitekturstudio hat seinen Sitz im Herzen von Detroit, Michigan. Es wurde 2018 von David Iannuzzi gegründet, einem Absolventen der Taubman School of Architecture an der University of Michigan, und widmet sich dem Design in einer Vielzahl von Maßstäben, darunter Wohnhäuser, Restaurants, zivile und künstlerische Räume sowie Gewerbegebäude.

Das Studio arbeitet mit verschiedenen Stilen und basiert auf umfangreicher Forschung und Kenntnis in Handwerk, Konstruktion und Materialien, was zu subtilen, eleganten und innovativen Designs führt, für die es bekannt ist. Mit großer Neugierde auf die Lebensstile und Bedürfnisse ihrer Kunden entwirft Iannuzzi Studio komfortable Räume, die durch ihre Bewohnung nur noch bereichert werden können.

IANNUZZI STUDIO

DAVID IANNUZZI

iannuzzistudio.com

Ce studio d'architecture et de design d'intérieur a ses bureaux au cœur de Détroit, dans le Michigan. Il a été fondé en 2018 par David Iannuzzi, diplômé de l'école d'architecture Taubman de l'université du Michigan, et se concentre sur la conception à différentes échelles, notamment des logements, des restaurants, des espaces civiques, artistiques et commerciaux.

Le cabinet travaille dans des styles variés, en s'appuyant sur une recherche et une connaissance approfondies de l'artisanat, de la construction et des matériaux, ce qui se traduit par des conceptions subtiles, élégantes et novatrices qui font sa renommée. Avec une profonde curiosité pour les styles de vie et les besoins de ses clients, Iannuzzi Studio conçoit des espaces confortables qui ne peuvent être enrichis qu'en étant habités.

Este estudio de arquitectura y diseño de interiores tiene sus oficinas en el corazón de Detroit, Michigan. Lo fundó en 2018 David Iannuzzi, egresado de la Escuela de Arquitectura Taubman de la Universidad de Michigan, y se dedica al diseño en una variedad de escalas, incluyendo viviendas, restaurantes, espacios cívicos, artísticos, y comerciales.

La firma trabaja con varios estilos, respaldada por una amplia investigación y conocimiento de la artesanía, la construcción y los materiales, lo que da lugar a diseños sutiles, elegantes e innovadores por los cuales es reconocida. Con una profunda curiosidad por los estilos de vida y necesidades de sus clientes, Iannuzzi Studio diseña espacios cómodos que solo pueden enriquecerse al ser habitados.

BRIARCLIFF

Michigan, United States

Photos © Rafael Gamo

Located in rural Franklin, this house combines an elegant form and façade with a dramatic and playful interior, making it the perfect space for a family with a passion for music and theatre.
The silhouette is inspired by the classic Michigan farmhouses, with their distinctive gabled roofs, but incorporates innovative materials and details. Four clearly delineated pavilions separate the private and public areas. The longest one spans the property from one end to the other, with exposed steel structures, large windows that open onto the pool and a wall of woodwork that provides privacy from the street. Complementing this main structure are eye-catching elements such as the sculptural fireplace in the living room and the kitchen in emerald green and walnut stained tones. The house is set into the topography with Corten steel retaining walls, so that from the street it appears hidden behind gentle hills. The effect encourages intimacy while revealing the playful character of the house as one approaches. The site design has respected the surrounding trees as much as possible.

Dieses Haus befindet sich in der ländlichen Umgebung von Franklin und vereint eine elegante Form und Fassade mit einem dramatischen und verspielten Inneren und wird somit zum idealen Raum für eine Familie, die sich für Musik und Theater begeistert.
Die Silhouette ist von den klassischen Farmhäusern in Michigan inspiriert, mit ihren charakteristischen Satteldächern, jedoch unter Verwendung innovativer Materialien und Details. Vier deutlich abgegrenzte Pavillons trennen die privaten Bereiche von den öffentlichen. Der längste Pavillon durchquert das Anwesen von einem Ende zum anderen und verfügt über sichtbare Stahlstrukturen, große Fenster, die sich zum Pool hin öffnen, und eine Wandverkleidung, die Privatsphäre von der Straße aus bietet. Zusätzlich zu dieser Hauptstruktur finden sich auffällige Elemente wie der skulpturale Kamin im Wohnzimmer und die Küche in Smaragdgrün und gefärbter Walnuss. Das Haus ist in die Topografie eingebettet und mit Cortenstahl-Stützwänden versehen, so dass es von der Straße aus hinter sanften Hügeln verborgen wirkt. Dieser Effekt fördert die Privatsphäre und enthüllt gleichzeitig den verspielten Charakter des Hauses, wenn man sich ihm nähert. Die Standortgestaltung hat die umgebenden Bäume weitestgehend respektiert.

Située dans la zone rurale de Franklin, cette maison allie une forme et une façade élégantes à un intérieur dramatique et ludique, devenant ainsi l'espace parfait pour une famille passionnée de musique et de théâtre.
Sa silhouette s'inspire des fermes classiques du Michigan, avec leurs toits caractéristiques à deux versants, tout en incorporant des matériaux et des détails innovants. Quatre pavillons clairement délimités séparent les zones privées des zones publiques. Le pavillon le plus long traverse la propriété d'un bout à l'autre, avec des structures en acier apparentes, de grandes baies vitrées s'ouvrant sur la piscine et un mur en menuiserie qui assure l'intimité depuis la rue. En complément de cette structure principale, des éléments saisissants apparaissent, tels que la cheminée sculpturale dans le salon et la cuisine aux tons verts émeraude et noyer teinté. La maison est nichée dans la topographie avec des murs de soutènement en acier corten, de sorte qu'elle semble cachée derrière de douces collines depuis la rue. Cet effet favorise l'intimité tout en révélant le caractère ludique de la maison à mesure que l'on s'approche. La conception du site a respecté au maximum les arbres environnants.

Ubicada en la zona rural de Franklin, esta casa combina una forma y fachada elegantes con un interior dramático y lúdico, convirtiéndose en el espacio perfecto para una familia apasionada por la música y el teatro.
La silueta se inspira en las clásicas granjas de Michigan, con sus característicos tejados a dos aguas, pero incorporando materiales y detalles innovadores. Cuatro pabellones claramente delimitados separan las áreas privadas de las públicas. El pabellón más largo atraviesa la propiedad de un extremo a otro, con estructuras de acero a la vista, amplios ventanales que se abren hacia la piscina y una pared con carpintería que brinda privacidad desde la calle. Complementando esta estructura principal, aparecen elementos llamativos como la chimenea escultural en el salón y la cocina en tonos verdes esmeralda y nogal teñido. La casa está enclavada en la topografía con muros de contención de acero corten, de manera que desde la calle parece escondida detrás de suaves colinas. El efecto favorece la intimidad a la vez que revela el carácter lúdico de la casa a medida que uno se acerca. El diseño del emplazamiento ha respetado al máximo los árboles circundantes.

The Mallorca-based studio is led by architect Jaime Salvá, and is identified by a contemporary Mediterranean architectural style, which prioritises local materials and geometries. After completing his architectural studies in Barcelona, the architect worked in San Francisco (USA) where he collaborated on the design of the private residence of film director George Lucas and office buildings in Silicon Valley, among other projects.

In 2006, he returned to Spain and founded his own studio. Since then, he has designed numerous projects for developers, investment funds and private clients, ranging from local families to elite sportsmen and international businessmen. Recently, the studio has expanded its frontiers, undertaking projects internationally.

Das auf Mallorca ansässige Studio wird von dem Architekten Jaime Salvá geleitet und zeichnet sich durch eine zeitgenössische mediterrane Architektur aus, die lokale Materialien und Geometrien betont. Nach Abschluss seines Architekturstudiums in Barcelona arbeitete der Architekt in San Francisco (USA), wo er an der Gestaltung der Privatresidenz des Filmregisseurs George Lucas und von Bürogebäuden im Silicon Valley mitwirkte, unter anderem an Projekten.

Im Jahr 2006 kehrte er nach Spanien zurück und gründete sein eigenes Studio. Seitdem hat er zahlreiche Projekte für Entwickler, Investmentfonds und private Kunden entworfen, darunter lokale Familien, Spitzensportler und internationale Unternehmer. Das Studio hat in jüngerer Zeit seine Grenzen erweitert und internationale Projekte realisiert.

JAIME SALVÁ
ARQUITECTURA & INTERIORISMO

JAIME SALVÁ

salvarq.com

Le cabinet basé à Majorque est dirigé par l'architecte Jaime Salvá et se distingue par un style architectural méditerranéen contemporain qui privilégie les matériaux locaux et les géométries. Après avoir terminé ses études d'architecture à Barcelone, l'architecte a travaillé à San Francisco (États-Unis), où il a collaboré à la conception de la résidence privée du réalisateur George Lucas et de bâtiments de bureaux dans la Silicon Valley, entre autres projets.

En 2006, il est retourné en Espagne et a fondé son propre cabinet. Depuis lors, il a conçu de nombreux projets pour des promoteurs, des fonds d'investissement et des clients particuliers, allant des familles locales aux athlètes de haut niveau et aux entrepreneurs internationaux. Récemment, le cabinet a étendu ses frontières en réalisant des projets à l'international.

El estudio con sede en Mallorca está dirigido por el arquitecto Jaime Salvá, y se caracteriza por un estilo arquitectónico mediterráneo contemporáneo, que prioriza los materiales locales y las geometrías. Después de completar sus estudios de arquitectura en Barcelona, el arquitecto trabajó en San Francisco (EEUU) donde colaboró en el diseño de la residencia privada del director de cine George Lucas y edificios de oficinas en Silicon Valley, entre otros proyectos.

En 2006, regresó a España y fundó su propio estudio. Desde entonces, ha diseñado numerosos proyectos para promotores, fondos de inversión y clientes particulares, que incluyen desde familias locales hasta deportistas de élite y empresarios internacionales. Recientemente, el estudio ha expandido sus fronteras, realizando proyectos a nivel internacional.

MORMAIQUEL HOUSE

Biniagual, Mallorca, Spain

Photos © Tomeu Canyellas

This rustic house located in a small village in the interior of Mallorca, is a detached single-family house on a plot of 35.000 m² with mountain views. Part of the plot is used as a vineyard for wine production. The house has been designed for a couple who enjoy the countryside and animals. It consists of a series of parallel walls that define the different areas. The layout of the rooms takes advantage of the best views and orientation, and maintains a connection to the rear for cross ventilation.
The design responds to a Mediterranean architectural style, with local materials such as masonry stone, extracted from the same plot. This stone is used both inside and outside the house. In the bathroom, micro-cement has been used on the vertical walls and in the bathtub cladding. The porch has a cane lattice roof, which contrasts with the white painted beams, providing a fresh, Mediterranean feel.
The owners were actively involved in the interior design, selecting the furniture and the kitchen.

Dieses rustikale Haus liegt in einem kleinen Dorf im Inland von Mallorca und ist ein freistehendes Einfamilienhaus auf einem 35.000 m² großen Grundstück mit Blick auf die Berge. Ein Teil des Grundstücks ist für einen Weinanbau zur Weinproduktion bestimmt. Das Haus wurde für ein Paar entworfen, das das Landleben und Tiere genießt. Es besteht aus einer Reihe paralleler Mauern, die die verschiedenen Bereiche definieren. Die Raumaufteilung nutzt die besten Ausblicke und Ausrichtungen und hält eine Verbindung zur Rückseite für Querlüftung aufrecht.
Das Design entspricht einer mediterranen Architektur mit lokalen Materialien wie Naturstein, der direkt vom Grundstück gewonnen wird. Dieser Stein wird sowohl im Innen- als auch im Außenbereich des Hauses verwendet. Im Badezimmer wurden Mikrozement an den vertikalen Wänden und an der Badewannenverkleidung verwendet. Die Veranda verfügt über ein Schilfdach, das im Kontrast zu den weiß gestrichenen Balken steht und ein frisches und mediterranes Gefühl vermittelt.
Die Eigentümer waren aktiv an der Innenraumgestaltung beteiligt und wählten Möbel und Küche aus.

Cette maison rustique située dans un petit village de l'intérieur de Majorque est une maison individuelle isolée sur un terrain de 35 000 m² avec vue sur les montagnes. Une partie du terrain est utilisée comme vignoble pour la production de vin. La maison a été conçue pour un couple qui aime la campagne et les animaux. Elle se compose d'une série de murs parallèles qui délimitent les différentes zones. La disposition des pièces profite des meilleures vues et de l'orientation, et maintient une connexion à l'arrière pour la ventilation transversale.
La conception répond à un style architectural méditerranéen, avec des matériaux locaux tels que la pierre de maçonnerie, extraite de la même parcelle. Cette pierre est utilisée aussi bien à l'intérieur qu'à l'extérieur de la maison. Dans la salle de bains, du microciment a été utilisé sur les parois verticales et dans le revêtement de la baignoire. Le porche a un toit en treillis de canne, qui contraste avec les poutres peintes en blanc, ce qui donne une impression de fraîcheur méditerranéenne.
Les propriétaires ont participé activement à l'aménagement intérieur, en choisissant le mobilier et la cuisine.

Esta vivienda rústica situada en un pequeño pueblo en el interior de Mallorca, es una casa unifamiliar aislada en una parcela de 35.000 m² con vistas a la montaña. Parte de la parcela se destina a una plantación de viñas para la producción de vino. La casa ha sido diseñada para una pareja que disfruta del campo y los animales. Se compone de una serie de muros paralelos que definen las diferentes áreas. La distribución de las habitaciones aprovecha las mejores vistas y orientación, y mantiene una conexión con la parte trasera para la ventilación cruzada.
El diseño responde a un estilo arquitectónico mediterráneo, con materiales locales como la piedra de mampostería, extraída de la misma parcela. Esta piedra se utiliza tanto en el interior como en el exterior de la vivienda. En el baño se ha utilizado microcemento en las paredes verticales y en el revestimiento de la bañera. El porche cuenta con un entramado de cañizo en el techo, que contrasta con las vigas pintadas de blanco, aportando una sensación fresca y mediterránea.
Los propietarios participaron activamente en el diseño de interiores, seleccionando los muebles y la cocina.

Juma Architects was founded in 2009 by Mathieu Luyens and Julie van De Keere, both architects who graduated from the Saint-Lucas Academy in Ghent. Before establishing their own studio, they both worked in studios in Antwerp and Ibiza. Juma's work is determined by a modern, minimalist aesthetic, emphasising the careful use of light, space, emotions and the unique characteristics of each place. Throughout the creative process, their projects incorporate multiple layers of detail, resulting in refined designs that highlight quality. The firm's goal is to carry out projects efficiently, from the early planning stages to the details of materials and furniture design. Their specific approach allows them to be both passionate designers and functional builders, creating cost-effective and personal structures.

Juma Architects wurde 2009 von Mathieu Luyens und Julie Van de Keere gegründet, beide Architektenabsolventen der Saint-Lucas-Akademie in Gent. Bevor sie ihr eigenes Studio gründeten, arbeiteten sie in Büros in Antwerpen und Ibiza. Die Arbeit von Juma zeichnet sich durch eine moderne und minimalistische Ästhetik aus, wobei besonderes Augenmerk auf die sorgfältige Nutzung von Licht, Raum, Emotionen und den einzigartigen Merkmalen jedes Ortes gelegt wird. Im kreativen Prozess integrieren ihre Projekte mehrere Schichten von Details, was zu raffinierten Designs führt, die Qualität betonen. Das Ziel des Studios ist es, Projekte effizient von den frühen Planungsphasen bis hin zu Materialdetails und Möbeldesign umzusetzen. Ihr spezifischer Ansatz ermöglicht es ihnen, sowohl leidenschaftliche Designer als auch funktionale Bauherren zu sein und kostengünstige und persönliche Strukturen zu schaffen.

JUMA ARCHITECTS

JULIE VAN DE KEERE, MATHIEU LUYENS

jumaarchitects.be

Juma Architects a été fondé en 2009 par Mathieu Luyens et Julie van De Keere, tous deux architectes diplômés de l'Académie Saint-Lucas de Gand. Avant de créer leur propre studio, ils ont tous deux travaillé dans des studios à Anvers et à Ibiza. Le travail de Juma se caractérise par une esthétique moderne et minimaliste, qui met l'accent sur l'utilisation prudente de la lumière, de l'espace, des émotions et des caractéristiques uniques de chaque lieu. Tout au long du processus créatif, leurs projets intègrent de multiples couches de détails, ce qui se traduit par des conceptions raffinées qui mettent l'accent sur la qualité. L'objectif du cabinet est de réaliser des projets de manière efficace, depuis les premières étapes de la planification jusqu'aux détails des matériaux et de la conception du mobilier. Leur approche spécifique leur permet d'être à la fois des concepteurs passionnés et des constructeurs fonctionnels, créant des structures rentables et personnelles.

Juma Architects fue fundado en 2009 por Mathieu Luyens y Julie van De Keere, ambos arquitectos graduados de la Academia Saint-Lucas en Gante. Antes de establecer su propio estudio, ambos trabajaron en estudios en Amberes e Ibiza. El trabajo de Juma se caracteriza por una estética moderna y minimalista, destacando el uso cuidadoso de la luz, el espacio, las emociones y las características únicas de cada lugar. A lo largo del proceso creativo, sus proyectos incorporan múltiples capas de detalle, resultando en diseños refinados que resaltan la calidad. El objetivo de la firma es llevar a cabo proyectos de manera eficiente, desde las primeras etapas de planificación hasta los detalles de los materiales y el diseño del mobiliario. Su enfoque específico les permite ser tanto apasionados diseñadores como constructores funcionales, creando estructuras rentables y personales.

FARMHOUSE CL

Deurle, Belgium

Photos © Annick Vernimmen

Juma Architects renovated a farmhouse in a village in the Flemish countryside, restoring its lost charm and improving interior comfort. Changes were made to the structure and roof height, gaining space and adding a storey with dormer windows that provide natural light and views, highlighting the rural character. The large exterior walls were insulated with environmentally friendly materials and plastered with lime. In addition, new arched windows in black wrought iron characteristic of this style were installed, which are combined with small openings arranged playfully along the wall.

The entrance door was integrated through a volume connecting the two wings of the house, with solid wooden beams supporting the new canopy. In the entrance hall, a new sculptural spiral staircase becomes the focal point, providing a warm sense of welcome. The kitchen was relocated to a central area of the property and the cooker was placed in the main fireplace.

An outbuilding where the kitchen was originally located was demolished to make way for a new timber volume that now houses the fitness room.

Juma Architects renovierte ein Bauernhaus in einem Dorf auf dem flämischen Land und verlieh ihm seinen verlorenen Charme zurück, während der Innenkomfort verbessert wurde. Es wurden Änderungen an der Struktur und Höhe des Dachs vorgenommen, um Platz zu gewinnen und eine Etage mit Dachfenstern hinzuzufügen, die natürliches Licht und Ausblicke bieten und den ländlichen Charakter betonen. Die großen äußeren Wände wurden mit ökologischen Materialien isoliert und mit Kalk verputzt. Darüber hinaus wurden neue Fenster in Form von schwarzen schmiedeeisernen Bögen installiert, die charakteristisch für diesen Stil sind und mit kleinen, spielerisch angeordneten Öffnungen entlang der Wand kombiniert werden.

Die Eingangstür wurde durch einen Volumen integriert, das die beiden Flügel des Hauses verbindet und von massiven Holzbalken getragen wird, die das neue Vordach stützen. Im Eingangsbereich wird eine neue und skulpturale Wendeltreppe zum Blickfang und vermittelt ein warmes Willkommensgefühl. Die Küche wurde in einen zentralen Bereich des Anwesens verlegt und der Herd in den Hauptkamin eingebaut.

Ein Anbau, in dem sich ursprünglich die Küche befand, wurde abgerissen, um Platz für ein neues Holzvolumen zu schaffen, das nun den Fitnessraum beherbergt.

Juma Architects a rénové une ferme dans un village de la campagne flamande, en lui redonnant son charme perdu et en améliorant le confort intérieur. Des modifications ont été apportées à la structure et à la hauteur du toit, ce qui a permis de gagner de l'espace et d'ajouter un étage avec des lucarnes qui apportent de la lumière naturelle et des vues, soulignant ainsi le caractère rural. Les grands murs extérieurs ont été isolés avec des matériaux écologiques et enduits de chaux. En outre, de nouvelles fenêtres cintrées en fer forgé noir, caractéristiques de ce style, ont été installées, combinées à de petites ouvertures disposées de manière ludique le long du mur.

La porte d'entrée a été intégrée à travers un volume reliant les deux ailes de la maison, avec des poutres en bois massif soutenant le nouvel auvent. Dans le hall d'entrée, un nouvel escalier en colimaçon sculptural devient le point central, offrant une sensation de bienvenue chaleureuse. La cuisine a été déplacée dans une zone centrale de la propriété et la cuisinière a été placée dans la cheminée principale.

Une dépendance où se trouvait à l'origine la cuisine a été démolie pour faire place à un nouveau volume en bois qui abrite aujourd'hui la salle de fitness.

Juma Architects renovó una granja en un pueblo de la campiña flamenca, devolviéndole su encanto perdido y mejorando el confort interior. Se realizaron cambios en la estructura y altura del tejado, ganando espacio y añadiendo una planta con ventanas abuhardilladas que brindan luz natural y vistas, resaltando el carácter rural. Los grandes muros exteriores se aislaron con materiales ecológicos y enlucidos con cal. Además, se instalaron nuevas ventanas en forma de arco en hierro forjado negro características de este estilo, las cuales se combinan con pequeñas aberturas dispuestas de forma lúdica a lo largo de la pared.

La puerta de entrada se integró a través de un volumen que conecta las dos alas de la casa, con vigas de madera maciza que sostienen la nueva marquesina. En el hall de entrada, una nueva y escultural escalera de caracol se convierte en el punto de atracción, brindando una cálida sensación de bienvenida. La cocina fue re ubicada en una zona central de la propiedad y la estufa se colocó en la chimenea principal.

Una construcción anexa donde originalmente se encontraba la cocina se demolió para dar paso a un nuevo volumen de madera que ahora alberga la sala de fitness.

Steve Kadlec is an architect and interior designer with over 30 years of experience in residential projects. In 2004 he founded his studio, forming a close-knit team that works closely with clients, contractors and suppliers to give each project the attention it deserves. His work focuses on client relationships and connection to place.

Kadlec's firm has been acknowledged with many awards over the years, including Luxe Red Awards and Modern Luxury distinctions, while his work is regularly featured in leading shelter publications, both locally and nationally. Although based in Chicago, his projects span the United States. Kadlec is an active member of various design organizations, and his firm supports several charities including DIFFA Chicago.

Steve Kadlec ist ein Architekt und Innenarchitekt mit über 30 Jahren Erfahrung in Wohnprojekten. Im Jahr 2004 gründete er sein Studio, das ein engagiertes Team bildet, das eng mit Kunden, Auftragnehmern und Lieferanten zusammenarbeitet, um jedem Projekt die Aufmerksamkeit zu geben, die es verdient. Seine Arbeit konzentriert sich auf die Kundenbeziehungen und die Verbindung zum Ort.

Das Kadlec-Studio wurde mit mehreren Preisen ausgezeichnet, darunter Luxe Red Awards und Auszeichnungen von Modern Luxury, und seine Arbeiten werden regelmäßig in renommierten Fachpublikationen veröffentlicht. Obwohl der Hauptsitz in Chicago liegt, erstrecken sich seine Projekte über die gesamten Vereinigten Staaten. Kadlec ist aktives Mitglied bedeutender Designorganisationen, und sein Unternehmen unterstützt verschiedene Wohltätigkeitsorganisationen in seiner Stadt einschließlich DIFFA Chicago..

KADLEC ARCHITECTURE + DESIGN

STEVE KADLEC

kadlecdesign.com

Steve Kadlec est un architecte et designer d'intérieur avec plus de 30 ans d'expérience dans les projets résidentiels. En 2004, il a fondé son studio, formant une équipe soudée qui travaille en étroite collaboration avec les clients, les entrepreneurs et les fournisseurs pour donner à chaque projet l'attention qu'il mérite. Son travail est axé sur les relations avec les clients et le lien avec le lieu.

L'entreprise de Kadlec a été récompensée par plusieurs prix au fil des années, notamment Luxe Red Awards et Modern Luxury distinctions, et son travail est régulièrement présenté dans des publications spécialisées de premier plan. Bien qu'elle soit basée à Chicago, ses projets couvrent l'ensemble des États-Unis. Kadlec est un membre actif des principales organisations de design, et son cabinet soutient plusieurs organisations caritatives dont le DIFFA Chicago.

Steve Kadlec es un arquitecto y diseñador de interiores con más de 30 años de experiencia en proyectos residenciales. En 2004 fundó su estudio, conformando un equipo unido que trabaja estrechamente con los clientes, contratistas y proveedores para dar a cada proyecto la atención que merece. Su trabajo se enfoca en las relaciones con los clientes y en la conexión con el lugar.

La firma de Kadlec ha sido reconocida con varios premios, incluyendo Luxe Red Awards y distinciones de Modern Luxury, a la vez que sus trabajos se publican asiduamente en destacadas publicaciones especializadas. Aunque su sede se encuentra en Chicago, sus proyectos se extienden por todo Estados Unidos. Kadlec es miembro activo de importantes organizaciones de diseño, y su empresa apoya a diversas organizaciones benéficas incluyendo el DIFFA Chicago

MICHIANA WEEKENDER

Indiana, United States

Photos © Tony Soluri

Steve Kadlec renovated this 1940´s cedar wood house, a haven of peace and nature he shares with his partner. The house was very well maintained, so the work focused on the interior design. The project respected the architecture and the rural setting, with a contemporary and laid-back casual aesthetic. Inspired by the casual elegance of California Craftsman style, the color palette is warm, eclectic and rustic. In a nod to the home's new personality, an Arne Jacobsen Egg chair stands out in the living room alongside a rustic-rooted coffee table and a Troscan daybed. In the dining room, leather chairs decorate a concrete table and deer antlers hang on the wall. In the solarium, a sofa upholstered in bouclé fabric combines with a Richard Wrightman lounger and petrified log tables.
In summer, the soul of the house is the covered porch that connects the interior to the lush gardens and wooded landscape. The screened porch opens onto a wooden deck that leads to a landscaped walkway and sun lounger overlooking the expansive lush lawn and wooded property.

Steve Kadlec hat dieses Zedernholzhaus aus den 1940er Jahren renoviert, eine Oase der Ruhe und der Natur, die er mit seinem Partner teilt. Das Haus war sehr gut erhalten, daher konzentrierte sich die Arbeit auf das Innendesign. Das Projekt respektierte die Architektur und die ländliche Umgebung und hatte eine zeitgenössische und entspannte Ästhetik. Inspiriert von der ungezwungenen Eleganz des kalifornischen Handwerkerstils ist die Farbpalette warm, eklektisch und rustikal. Als Hinweis auf die neue Persönlichkeit des Hauses ragt ein Egg Chair von Arne Jacobsen im Wohnzimmer neben einem rustikalen Wurzelholz-Couchtisch und einem Troscan-Schlafsofa heraus. Im Esszimmer schmücken Ledersessel einen Betontisch und Hirschgeweihe hängen an der Wand. Im Wintergarten passt ein in Bouclé-Stoff gepolstertes Sofa zu einem Richard Wrightman-Liegestuhl und versteinerten Baumstamm-Tischen.
Im Sommer ist die überdachte Veranda das Herzstück des Hauses und verbindet den Innenraum mit den üppigen Gärten und der bewaldeten Landschaft. Die überdachte Veranda führt zu einer Holzterrasse, die zu einem Gartenweg und Sonnenliegen mit Blick auf den üppigen Rasen und das bewaldete Grundstück führt.

Steve Kadlec a rénové cette maison en cèdre des années 1940, un havre de paix et de nature qu'il partage avec sa compagne. La maison étant très bien entretenue, les travaux se sont concentrés sur l'aménagement intérieur. Le projet a respecté l'architecture et le cadre rural, avec une esthétique contemporaine et décontractée. Inspirée par l'élégance décontractée du style Craftsman californien, la palette de couleurs est chaleureuse, éclectique et rustique. En clin d'œil à la nouvelle personnalité de la maison, une chaise Egg d'Arne Jacobsen trône dans le salon aux côtés d'une table basse aux racines rustiques et d'un lit de jour Troscan. Dans la salle à manger, des chaises en cuir décorent une table en béton et des bois de cerf sont accrochés au mur. Dans le solarium, un canapé recouvert de tissu bouclé est associé à une chaise longue Richard Wrightman et à des tables en bois pétrifié.
En été, l'âme de la maison est le porche couvert qui relie l'intérieur aux jardins luxuriants et au paysage boisé. Le porche couvert s'ouvre sur une terrasse en bois menant à une allée de jardin et à des chaises longues donnant sur la pelouse luxuriante et le terrain boisé.

Steve Kadlec renovó esta casa de madera de cedro de 1940, un remanso de paz y naturaleza que comparte con su pareja. La casa estaba muy bien mantenida, así que el trabajo se centró en el diseño de interiores. El proyecto respetó la arquitectura y el entorno rural, con una estética contemporánea y desenfadada. Inspirada en la elegancia informal del estilo artesano californiano, la paleta de colores es cálida, ecléctica y rústica. Como indicio de la nueva personalidad de la casa, una silla Egg de Arne Jacobsen destaca en el salón junto a una mesa de centro de raíz rústica y un sofá cama Troscan. En el comedor, las sillas de piel decoran una mesa de hormigón y unas astas de ciervo cuelgan en la pared. En el solárium, un sofá tapizado en tela bouclé combina con una tumbona Richard Wrightman y mesas de tronco petrificado.
En verano, el alma de la casa es el porche cubierto que conecta el interior con los exuberantes jardines y el paisaje boscoso. El porche cubierto se abre a una terraza de madera que conduce a un camino ajardinado y a tumbonas con vistas al frondoso césped y a la parcela arbolada.

Founded in 2002 by Charlie Lazor, Lazor/Office is a dynamic design studio committed to creating spaces that improve people's quality of life. The firm prioritizes the development of sensitive and integrated responses to the places in which it works.

Interdisciplinary in nature, Lazor/Office has resisted specializing in one particular aspect of design. The office deals with a wide range of residential, commercial and theoretical projects, ranging in scope from furniture to architecture to building systems.

Charlie Lazor also teaches and lectures at various academic institutions and has been a guest juror at some of America's best architecture schools. He is also co-founder of Blu Dot furniture and creator of the FlatPak House system.

Lazor/Office wurde 2002 von Charlie Lazor gegründet und ist ein dynamisches Designstudio, das sich darauf konzentriert, Räume zu schaffen, die die Lebensqualität der Menschen verbessern. Das Unternehmen legt Wert auf die Schaffung von Räumen und die Entwicklung sensibler und integrierter Lösungen für die Orte, an denen es arbeitet.

Als interdisziplinäres Studio hat Lazor/Office sich dagegen gewehrt, sich auf einen bestimmten Aspekt des Designs zu spezialisieren. Das Büro beschäftigt sich mit einer breiten Palette von Wohn-, Gewerbe- und theoretischen Projekten, die von Möbeln über Architektur bis hin zu Baukonstruktionen reichen.

Charlie Lazor ist auch Professor und Vortragender an verschiedenen akademischen Institutionen und war Gastjuror an renommierten Architekturschulen. Darüber hinaus ist er Mitbegründer von Blu Dot Furniture und Schöpfer des FlatPak House-Systems.

LAZOR/OFFICE

CHARLIE LAZOR

lazoroffice.com

Fondé en 2002 par Charlie Lazor, Lazor/Office est un studio de design dynamique qui se consacre à la création d'espaces qui améliorent la qualité de vie des gens. L'entreprise donne la priorité à la création d'espaces et au développement de réponses sensibles et intégrées aux lieux dans lesquels elle travaille.

De nature interdisciplinaire, Lazor/Office ne s'est pas spécialisé dans un aspect particulier de la conception. Le bureau s'occupe d'un large éventail de projets résidentiels, commerciaux et théoriques, allant du mobilier à l'architecture en passant par les systèmes de construction.

Charlie Lazor enseigne et donne des conférences dans diverses institutions académiques et a été juré invité dans quelques-unes des meilleures écoles d'architecture des États-Unis. Il est également cofondateur de Blu Dot furniture et créateur du système FlatPak House.

Fundado en 2002 por Charlie Lazor, Lazor/Office es un estudio de diseño dinámico comprometido con la creación de espacios que mejoren la calidad de vida de las personas. La firma da prioridad a la creación de espacios y al desarrollo de respuestas sensibles e integradas a los lugares en los que trabaja.

De naturaleza interdisciplinar, Lazor/Office se ha resistido a especializarse en un aspecto concreto del diseño. La oficina se ocupa de una amplia gama de proyectos residenciales, comerciales y teóricos, con un alcance que varía desde el mobiliario hasta la arquitectura y los sistemas de construcción.

Charlie Lazor también es profesor y conferencista en diversas instituciones académicas y ha sido jurado invitado en algunas de las mejores escuelas de arquitectura de Estados Unidos. Además, es cofundador de Blu Dot furniture y creador del sistema FlatPak House.

SILHOUETTE HOUSE

Montana, United States

Photos © Jasper Lazor Photos

The owners were looking for a place by the river to enjoy their passion for fly fishing. They commissioned the construction of a house that put them in touch with the natural environment in the company of friends.
The house has two enclosed sections connected by a system of outdoor decks and walkways. In silhouette it resembles a Montana homesteader's barn clad with wooden planks, a metal roof, rustic doors, and hatches for ventilation. On closer inspection, however, the house has unusual features.
Defined by minimalist surfaces and clean geometries, it has a contemporary feel with a cozy touch. The douglas fir structure is exposed and in-filled with glass, creating the feeling of a room within nature. The living room, kitchen, and dining area occupy the ground floor of one side of the house. Overhead, a lofted game room has long views of the river and the mountains. In the other volume are the bedrooms: bunk rooms for guests are below, while bedrooms with large skylights for stargazing are above.

Die Eigentümer waren auf der Suche nach einem Ort am Fluss, um ihrer Leidenschaft für das Fliegenfischen nachzugehen. Sie gaben den Bau eines Hauses in Auftrag, das sie in Gesellschaft von Freunden mit der Natur in Kontakt bringt.
Das Haus besteht aus zwei miteinander verbundenen Volumen, die durch Dächer und Gehwege verbunden sind und der typischen Struktur von Scheunen in Montana ähneln: mit Holzbrettern verkleidet, mit Metall bedachtes Dach, Holzklappen zur Belüftung und ohne Verschlüsse. Bei genauerer Betrachtung weist das Haus jedoch ungewöhnliche Merkmale auf.
Im Haus dominieren minimalistische Oberflächen und klare Geometrien, die eine zeitgenössische Atmosphäre mit gemütlicher Note vermitteln. Die Holzstrukturteile sind mit Glas gefüllt und erzeugen das Gefühl eines Raums in der Natur. Im Erdgeschoss eines der Volumen befinden sich das Wohnzimmer, die Küche und der Essbereich. Im Obergeschoss gibt es einen Spielraum mit Blick auf den Fluss und die Berge. Im anderen Volumen befinden sich die Schlafzimmer, wobei die Schlafzimmer im Obergeschoss große Dachfenster haben, um die Sterne zu betrachten.

Les propriétaires cherchaient un endroit au bord de la rivière pour profiter de leur passion pour la pêche à la mouche, et ont commandé la construction d'une maison pour être en contact avec l'environnement en compagnie d'amis.
La maison se compose de deux parties reliées par un système de terrasses et de passerelles. Sa silhouette ressemble à la structure typique des granges du Montana : revêtement en planches de bois, toit en métal, portes en bois pour la ventilation et absence d'enceintes. En y regardant de plus près, la maison présente toutefois des caractéristiques inhabituelles.
La maison est dominée par des surfaces minimalistes et des géométries épurées qui lui confèrent un aspect contemporain avec une touche chaleureuse. Les éléments structurels en bois sont remplis de verre, ce qui donne l'impression d'une pièce dans la nature. Au rez-de-chaussée de l'un des volumes se trouvent le salon, la cuisine et la salle à manger. À l'étage supérieur, une salle de jeux offre une vue sur la rivière et les montagnes. Dans l'autre volume se trouvent les chambres à coucher ; celles de l'étage supérieur sont dotées de grandes lucarnes permettant d'observer les étoiles.

Los dueños buscaban un lugar junto al rio para disfrutar de su pasión por la pesca con mosca, y encargaron la construcción de una casa para estar en contacto con el entorno en compañía de amigos.
La casa tiene dos cuerpos conectados a través de un sistema de cubiertas y pasarelas. Su silueta se asemeja a la estructura típica de los graneros de Montana: revestida con tablones de madera, techo metálico, compuertas de madera para la ventilación y ausencia de cerramientos. Sin embargo, al observarla detenidamente, la vivienda presenta características inusuales.
En la casa dominan las superficies minimalistas y las geometrías limpias que otorgan una sensación contemporánea con un toque acogedor. Los elementos estructurales de madera tienen paredes de cristal creando la sensación de una habitación dentro de la naturaleza. En la planta baja de uno de los volúmenes se encuentran el salón, la cocina y el comedor. En la planta superior, hay una sala de juegos con vistas al río y a las montañas. En el otro volumen están las habitaciones; las de la planta superior cuentan con amplios tragaluces para contemplar las estrellas.

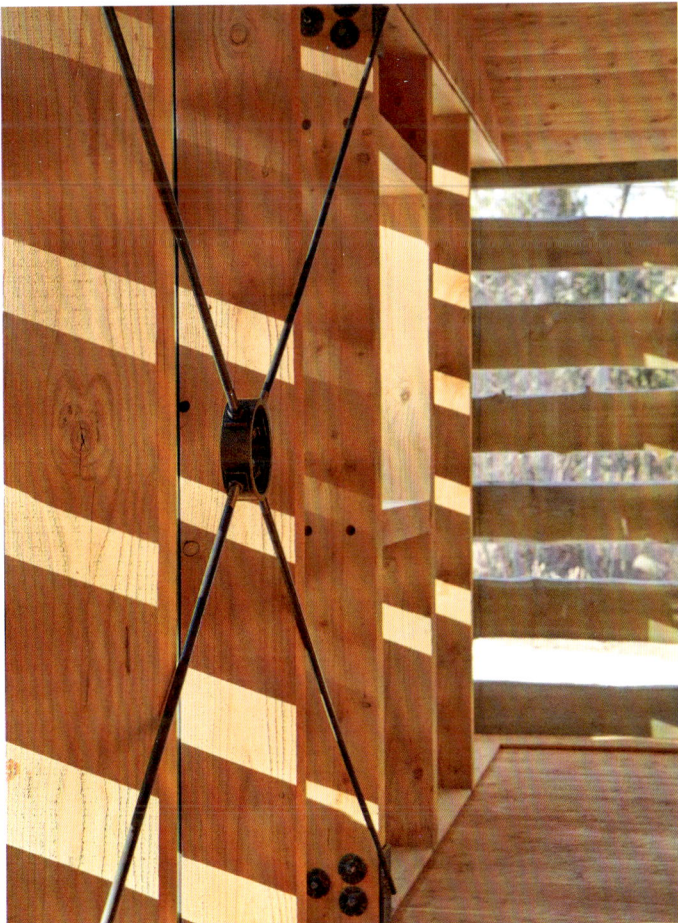

Miller Roodell Architects, an architectural firm based in Bozeman, Montana, is dedicated to capturing the essence of the American West with exceptional designs that incorporate sustainable strategies. Whether it's a traditional residence, a modern retreat or a commercial project, the firm is dedicated to ensuring that its projects have a positive impact on the communities it serves.

Joe Roodell, principal and founding member, draws inspiration from vernacular style and creates designs that blend into their surroundings. Matt Miller, also a principal and founder, embraces simplicity and a strong connection to nature in his work philosophy. Both Joe and Matt hold Master of Architecture degrees from Montana State University and are licensed in several states.

Miller Roodell Architects, ein Architekturbüro mit Sitz in Bozeman, Montana, hat es sich zur Aufgabe gemacht, die Essenz des amerikanischen Westens mit außergewöhnlichen Entwürfen einzufangen, die nachhaltige Strategien beinhalten. Ob traditionelles Wohnhaus, moderner Rückzugsort oder kommerzielles Projekt, das Büro ist bestrebt, positive Auswirkungen auf die Gemeinschaften zu erzielen, die es bedient.

Joe Roodell, Direktor und Mitbegründer, lässt sich vom landestypischen Stil inspirieren und entwirft Designs, die sich in die Umgebung integrieren. Matt Miller, ebenfalls Direktor und Mitbegründer, verfolgt in seiner Arbeitsphilosophie die Prinzipien der Einfachheit und einer starken Verbindung zur Natur. Sowohl Joe als auch Matt haben einen Master-Abschluss in Architektur von der Montana State University und sind in verschiedenen Bundesstaaten lizenziert.

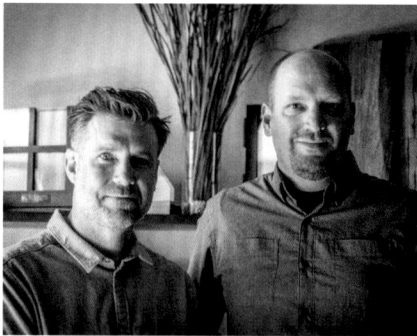

MILLER ROODELL ARCHITECTS

JOE ROODELL, MATT MILLER

miller-roodell.com

Miller Roodell Architects, un cabinet d'architectes basé à Bozeman, dans le Montana, s'attache à capturer l'essence de l'Ouest américain grâce à des conceptions exceptionnelles qui intègrent des stratégies durables. Qu'il s'agisse d'une résidence traditionnelle, d'une retraite moderne ou d'un projet commercial, le cabinet s'attache à faire en sorte que ses projets aient un impact positif sur les communautés qu'il dessert.

Joe Roodell, directeur et membre fondateur, s'inspire du style vernaculaire et crée des projets qui s'intègrent dans leur environnement. Matt Miller, également directeur et membre fondateur, adopte la simplicité et un lien étroit avec la nature dans sa philosophie de travail. Joe et Matt sont tous deux titulaires d'une maîtrise en architecture de l'université d'État du Montana et sont agréés dans plusieurs États.

Miller Roodell Architects, un estudio de arquitectura con sede en Bozeman, Montana, que se dedica a captar la esencia del Oeste americano con diseños excepcionales que incorporan estrategias sostenibles. Ya sea una residencia tradicional, un refugio moderno o un proyecto comercial, el estudio está abocado a que sus proyectos tengan un impacto positivo en las comunidades a las que sirve.

Joe Roodell, director y miembro fundador, se inspira en el estilo vernáculo y crea diseños que se integran en el entorno. Matt Miller, también director y fundador, adopta la simplicidad y una fuerte conexión con la naturaleza en su filosofía de trabajo. Tanto Joe como Matt tienen un máster en arquitectura de la Montana State University y están autorizados en varios Estados.

ROCKY MOUNTAIN RECLAIMED BARN

Stanley, Idaho, United States

Photos © Lucy Call

This house is a former barn that was dismantled in New York's Hudson Valley and rebuilt in Idaho's Saw-tooth Mountains. It is a "New World Dutch Barn", which is the American name for a type of barn. The place reflects the family's close connection to this land as a mountain retreat. The dwelling bears witness to the Revolutionary War and shows the craftsmanship of its owners. Next to this barn, there is another one for bicycles, built with reclaimed wood and equipped with a washing area.
The house offers options for relaxing outdoors. It has a patio for breakfast and a large terrace to admire the mountain. In addition, there is a porch with a fireplace and a covered porch for family and friends gatherings. The interior features authentic barn features and eclectic furnishings. The reborn materials have imperfections that tell their own stories. The owners spent years searching for unique furnishings to complement this one-of-a-kind home. The purpose of this dwelling is to preserve authenticity, promote sustainability and pay homage to the mountain environment.

Dieses Haus ist eine umgebaute Scheune, die im Hudson Valley in New York demontiert und in den Saw-tooth-Bergen in Idaho wieder aufgebaut wurde. Es handelt sich um eine „New World Dutch Barn", wie dieser Scheunentyp in den USA genannt wird. Der Ort spiegelt die enge Verbindung wider, die die Familie mit die-sem Land als Zufluchtsort in den Bergen hat. Das Haus ist Zeuge des Unabhängigkeitskrieges und zeigt das handwerkliche Geschick seiner Besitzer. Neben dieser Scheune gibt es eine weitere Scheune für Fahrräder, die aus wiederverwendetem Holz gebaut ist und über einen Waschbereich verfügt.
Das Haus bietet Möglichkeiten zum Entspannen im Freien. Es verfügt über einen Frühstückspatio und eine große Terrasse, um die Berge zu bewundern. Darüber hinaus gibt es eine Veranda mit Kamin und eine über-dachte Veranda für Familien- und Freundestreffen. Das Innere präsentiert authentische Scheunenelemente und eklektische Möbel. Die wiederverwendeten Materialien weisen Unvollkommenheiten auf, die ihre eige-nen Geschichten erzählen. Die Besitzer haben Jahre damit verbracht, einzigartige Möbelstücke zu suchen, um dieses einzigartige Zuhause zu ergänzen. Der Zweck dieser Behausung besteht darin, Authentizität zu bewahren, Nachhaltigkeit zu fördern und der Berglandschaft Tribut zu zollen.

Cette maison est une ancienne grange qui a été démontée dans la vallée de l'Hudson à New York et recons-truite dans les montagnes Sawtooth de l'Idaho. Il s'agit d'une « New World Dutch Barn », nom américain d'un type de grange. L'endroit reflète le lien étroit que la famille entretient avec cette terre en tant que lieu de retraite en montagne. L'habitation témoigne de la guerre d'Indépendance et montre le savoir-faire de ses propriétaires. À côté de cette grange, il y a une autre grange pour les vélos, construite avec du bois de récupération et équipée d'une aire de lavage.
La maison offre des possibilités de se détendre à l'extérieur. Elle dispose d'un patio pour le petit-déjeuner et d'une grande terrasse pour admirer la montagne. En outre, il y a un porche avec une cheminée et un porche couvert pour les réunions avec la famille et les amis. L'intérieur présente des éléments de grange authentiques et un mobilier éclectique. Les matériaux récupérés présentent des imperfections qui ra-content leur propre histoire. Les propriétaires ont passé des années à chercher des meubles uniques pour compléter cette maison unique en son genre. L'objectif de cette demeure est de préserver l'authenticité, de promouvoir le développement durable et de rendre hommage à l'environnement montagnard.

Esta casa es un antiguo granero que se desmonto en el valle neoyorquino del Hudson y se reconstruyó en las montañas Sawtooth de Idaho. Se trata de un «New World Dutch Barn» que es el nombre que se da en Estados Unidos a un tipo de granero. El lugar refleja el estrecho vínculo que la familia tiene con esta tierra como refugio en las montañas. La vivienda es testigo de la Guerra de la Independencia y muestra la habili-dad artesanal de sus propietarios. Junto a este granero, hay otro destinado a las bicicletas, construido con maderas recuperadas y equipado con una zona de lavado
La casa ofrece opciones para relajarse al aire libre. Cuenta con un patio para desayunar y una amplia terra-za para admirar la montaña. Además, tiene un porche con chimenea y otro porche cubierto para reuniones familiares y con amigos. El interior presenta auténticos elementos de granero y mobiliario ecléctico. Los materiales recuperados presentan imperfecciones que cuentan sus propias historias. Los propietarios pa-saron años buscando muebles únicos para complementar esta vivienda única. El propósito de esta morada es preservar la autenticidad, fomentar la sostenibilidad y rendir homenaje al entorno montañoso.

Presicci + Pantanella D'Ettorre Architetti is a studio founded by architects Valeria Presicci and Carlo Pantanella D'Ettorre in 2019 in Orbetello. Their approach is based on research and draws on the sensibility acquired in international architecture studios. Their projects focus on investigating each location and establishing relationships between the historical and the contemporary, showing a deep concern for the environment. Their design process ranges from large to small scale, and seeks a sustainable and balanced architecture, focusing on the interior vocation of places and the creation of spaces for the wellbeing of the people who inhabit them. They pay special attention to context, and consider constraints as creative opportunities rather than obstacles.

Presicci + Pantanella D'Ettorre Architetti ist ein Studio, das von den Architekten Valeria Presicci und Carlo Pantanella D'Ettorre 2019 in Orbetello gegründet wurde. Ihr Ansatz basiert auf Forschung und nährt sich von der Sensibilität, die sie in internationalen Architekturstudios entwickelt haben. Ihre Projekte konzentrieren sich darauf, jeden Standort zu erforschen und Beziehungen zwischen Historischem und Zeitgenössischem herzustellen, wobei sie eine tiefe Sorge um die Umwelt zeigen. Ihr Designprozess umfasst sowohl große als auch kleine Maßstäbe und strebt eine nachhaltige und ausgewogene Architektur an, die sich auf die innere Bestimmung der Orte konzentriert und Räume schafft, die das Wohlbefinden der Menschen, die sie bewohnen, priorisieren. Sie legen besonderen Wert auf den Kontext und betrachten Einschränkungen als kreative Möglichkeiten anstelle von Hindernissen.

© Yasser Lashin

PRESICCI + PANTANELLA D'ETTORRE ARCHITETTI

VALERIA PRESICCI, CARLO PANTANELLA D'ETTORRE

ppdarchitetti.it

Presicci + Pantanella D'Ettorre Architetti est un studio fondé par les architectes Valeria Presicci et Carlo Pantanella D'Ettorre en 2019 à Orbetello. Leur approche est basée sur la recherche et s'appuie sur la sensibilité acquise dans les studios d'architecture internationaux. Leurs projets se concentrent sur l'étude de chaque lieu et l'établissement de relations entre l'historique et le contemporain, tout en montrant une profonde préoccupation pour l'environnement. Leur processus de conception s'étend de la grande à la petite échelle et recherche une architecture durable et équilibrée, en se concentrant sur la vocation intérieure des lieux et la création d'espaces qui privilégient le bien-être des personnes qui les habitent. Ils accordent une attention particulière au contexte et considèrent les contraintes comme des opportunités créatives plutôt que comme des obstacles.

Presicci + Pantanella D'Ettorre Architetti es un estudio fundado por los arquitectos Valeria Presicci y Carlo Pantanella D'Ettorre en 2019 en Orbetello. Su enfoque se basa en la investigación y se nutre de la sensibilidad adquirida en estudios de arquitectura internacionales. Sus proyectos se centran en investigar cada ubicación y establecer relaciones entre lo histórico y lo contemporáneo, mostrando una profunda preocupación por el medio ambiente. Su proceso de diseño abarca desde la escala grande hasta la pequeña, y busca una arquitectura sostenible y equilibrada, centrada en la vocación interior de los lugares y en la creación de espacios que prioricen el bienestar de las personas que los habitan. Prestan especial atención al contexto, y consideran las limitaciones como oportunidades creativas en lugar de obstáculos.

PODERE 62

San Donato, Grosseto, Italy

Photos © Lorenzo Zandri

Podere 62 is located in the countryside of San Donato in Tuscany. The building is one of a series of farms built in the 1930s as part of a reclamation project for marshland in the lower Maremma. The main building is on two levels, with a rectangular ground plan and a central masonry spine that divides it lengthwise. Next to it is a single-storey annex that was used as a barn and shed and now is also part of the house. The intervention sought to renovate the entire complex to recover the Tuscan rural component and adapt it to the needs of a couple and their children who moved from London.

The two main principles were to improve energy efficiency and restore the original architectural identity. The rooms are arranged in a continuum, with shared and private spaces connected to each other. Terraces on the first floor offer views of the landscape. Both the exterior and interior of the farmhouse are identified by the use of natural local materials and defined geometric forms, such as travertine window frames, terracotta exterior paving, arches and wooden furniture.

Podere 62 befindet sich auf dem Land von San Donato in der Toskana. Das Gebäude ist Teil einer Reihe von Bauernhöfen, die in den 1930er Jahren im Rahmen eines Projekts zur Wiederherstellung von Sumpfgebieten in der unteren Maremma errichtet wurden. Das Hauptgebäude hat zwei Stockwerke mit einem rechteckigen Grundriss und einem zentralen Mauerwerk, das es längs teilt. Daneben befindet sich ein einstöckiges Nebengebäude, das als Scheune und Schuppen genutzt wurde und nun ebenfalls Teil des Hauses ist. Die Renovierung zielte darauf ab, die gesamte Anlage wiederherzustellen und an die Bedürfnisse eines Paares und ihrer Kinder anzupassen, die von London dorthin gezogen sind.

Die beiden Hauptziele waren die Verbesserung der Energieeffizienz und die Wiederherstellung der ursprünglichen architektonischen Identität. Die Räume sind kontinuierlich angeordnet, wobei Gemeinschafts- und Privaträume miteinander verbunden sind. Die Terrassen im ersten Stock bieten einen Blick auf die Landschaft. Sowohl das Äußere als auch das Innere des Bauernhofs zeichnen sich durch die Verwendung von natürlichen lokalen Materialien und definierten geometrischen Formen aus, wie z.B. die Travertinrahmen an den Fenstern, der Terrakottaboden im Außenbereich, die Bögen und das Holzmobiliar.

Le Podere 62 est situé dans la campagne de San Donato, en Toscane. Le bâtiment fait partie d'une série de fermes construites dans les années 1930 dans le cadre d'un projet de mise en valeur des marais de la basse Maremme. Le bâtiment principal est sur deux niveaux, avec un plan rectangulaire et une colonne centrale en maçonnerie qui le divise dans le sens de la longueur. À côté se trouve une annexe de plain-pied qui servait de grange et de remise et qui fait maintenant partie de la maison. L'intervention visait à rénover l'ensemble du complexe pour récupérer la composante rurale toscane et l'adapter aux besoins d'un couple et de leurs enfants qui ont déménagé de Londres.

Les deux principaux objectifs étaient d'améliorer l'efficacité énergétique et de restaurer l'identité architecturale d'origine. Les pièces sont disposées en continuum, avec des espaces partagés et privés reliés les uns aux autres. Les terrasses du premier étage offrent des vues sur le paysage. L'extérieur et l'intérieur de la ferme se caractérisent par l'utilisation de matériaux naturels locaux et de formes géométriques définies, comme les encadrements de fenêtres en travertin, le pavage extérieur en terre cuite, les arches et le mobilier en bois.

Podere 62 se ubica en la campiña de San Donato en la Toscana. La edificación forma parte de una serie de granjas construidas en la década de 1930 como parte de un proyecto de recuperación de zonas pantanosas en la baja Maremma. El edificio principal tiene dos niveles, con una planta rectangular y una espina central de mampostería que lo divide longitudinalmente. Junto a él se encuentra un anexo de una sola planta que se utilizó como granero y cobertizo y ahora también forma parte de la casa. La intervención buscó renovar todo el complejo para recuperar el componente rural toscano y adaptarlo a las necesidades de una pareja y sus hijos que se mudaron desde Londres.

Los dos objetivos principales fueron mejorar la eficiencia energética y restaurar la identidad arquitectónica original. Las habitaciones se organizan de forma continua, con espacios compartidos y privados conectados entre sí. Las terrazas en el primer piso ofrecen vistas del paisaje. Tanto el exterior como el interior de la granja se caracterizan por el uso de materiales locales naturales y formas geométricas definidas, como los marcos de travertino en las ventanas, el pavimento exterior de terracota, los arcos y los muebles de madera.

Rita Donahoe, owner and principal designer of Rita Chan Interiors, works in high-end residential design, from furnishings to large-scale renovations and building homes from the ground up. Her work creates calm, intimate spaces connected to nature, with a focus on a clean, natural aesthetic. Her company was established in 2013 and is based in Santa Barbara.

Rob Maday, meanwhile, is an honours graduate in Landscape Architecture from Cal Poly SLO, and established his firm in 2009. His firm Boskyland focuses on creating landscapes aligned with California's climate and culture. Architect Dylan Henderson, with degrees from the University of Southern California and the University of California, Berkeley, established his architecture practice Salt Architecture in Santa Barbara in 2013. In his work, a connection to nature and art is evident.

Rita Donahoe, Inhaberin und leitende Designerin von Rita Chan Interiors, ist auf hochwertiges Wohndesign spezialisiert, von Möbeln über umfassende Renovierungen bis hin zum Neubau von Häusern. Ihre Arbeit schafft ruhige und intime Räume, die mit der Natur verbunden sind und sich auf eine saubere und natürliche Ästhetik konzentrieren. Ihr Unternehmen wurde 2013 gegründet und hat seinen Sitz in Santa Barbara.

Rob Maday ist Absolvent mit Auszeichnung in Landschaftsarchitektur von der Cal Poly SLO und gründete sein Unternehmen 2009. Seine Firma Boskyland konzentriert sich auf die Gestaltung von Landschaften, die im Einklang mit dem Klima und der Kultur Kaliforniens stehen. Der Architekt Dylan Henderson, mit Abschlüssen von der University of Southern California und der University of California, Berkeley, gründete sein Architekturstudio Salt Architecture 2013 in Santa Barbara. In seiner Arbeit zeigt sich die Verbindung zur Natur und zur Kun.

RITA CHAN INTERIORS, BOSKYLAND, SALT ARCHITECTURE

RITA DONAHOE, ROB MADAY, DYLAN HENDERSON

ritachaninteriors.com - boskyland.com - saltchitect.com

Rita Donahoe, propriétaire et designer principale de Rita Chan Interiors, est spécialisée dans la conception résidentielle haut de gamme, de l'ameublement aux rénovations à grande échelle, en passant par la construction de maisons à partir de zéro. Les projets du cabinet créent des espaces calmes et intimes en lien avec la nature, en mettant l'accent sur une esthétique épurée et naturelle. Son entreprise a été créée en 2013 et est basée à Santa Barbara.

Rob Maday, quant à lui, est diplômé avec mention en architecture paysagère de Cal Poly SLO, et a créé son entreprise en 2009. Les projets de son atelier Boskyland sont axés sur la création de paysages adaptés au climat et à la culture de la Californie. L'architecte Dylan Henderson, diplômé de l'université de Californie du Sud et de l'université de Californie à Berkeley, a créé son cabinet d'architecture, Salt Architecture, à Santa Barbara en 2013. Son travail montre un lien avec la nature et l'art.

Rita Donahoe, propietaria y diseñadora principal de Rita Chan Interiors, se especializa en diseño residencial de alta gama, desde mobiliario hasta renovaciones a gran escala y construcción de viviendas desde cero. Su trabajo crea espacios tranquilos e íntimos conectados con la naturaleza, centrándose en una estética limpia y natural. Su empresa fue creada en 2013 y tiene su sede en Santa Bárbara.

Rob Maday, por su parte, es graduado con honores en Arquitectura del Paisaje en Cal Poly SLO, y estableció su empresa en 2009. Los proyectos de su firma Boskyland, se centran en crear paisajes alineados con el clima y la cultura de California. El arquitecto Dylan Henderson, con títulos de la Universidad del Sur de California y la Universidad de California, Berkeley, estableció su estudio de arquitectura, Salt Architecture, en Santa Bárbara en 2013. En sus trabajos se aprecia la conexión con la naturaleza y el arte.

ROLLING VINES RANCH

Santa Ynez, California, United States

Photos © Gavin Carter

Surrounded by vineyards and century-old oak trees, this 1970s home is the result of a complete renovation by interior designer Rita Chan, landscaped architect Rob Maday and architect Dylan Henderson. The property includes the main house, a guest house, an office and a building with a guest flat and wine cellar. The new design brought new life and appearance without losing the original vernacular architecture. The designers gave it a modern and clean, yet rustic and natural style. The inspiration has been the environment, so the colour palette assumes soothing neutrals with touches of green and earth on a white background.
In the interior, vintage and modern coexist. The pieces of furniture were commissioned by local craftsmen linked to the grape harvest. Of particular note is the recovery of wood from a barn and the old cupboards and worktops of the previous owner who manufactured horse-drawn carriages and equestrian equipment.
In the outdoor spaces, rural-inspired gardens were created, with sheltered views and gathering spaces to be enjoyed in both summer and winter.

Umgeben von Weinbergen und jahrhundertealten Eichen ist dieses Haus von 1970 das Ergebnis einer umfassenden Renovierung durch die Innenarchitektin Rita Chan, den Landschaftsarchitekten Rob Maday und den Architekten Dylan Henderson. Das Anwesen umfasst das Haupthaus, ein Gästehaus, ein Büro und ein Gebäude mit Gästeapartments und Weinkeller. Das neue Design verlieh dem Haus neues Leben und Erscheinungsbild, ohne die ursprüngliche einheimische Architektur zu verlieren. Die Designer verliehen ihm einen modernen und sauberen Stil, der gleichzeitig rustikal und natürlich ist. Die Inspiration kam aus der Umgebung, daher verwendet die Farbpalette beruhigende neutrale Töne mit grünen und erdigen Akzenten auf weißem Hintergrund.
Im Inneren vereinen sich Vintage und Moderne. Die Möbelstücke wurden von örtlichen Handwerkern und Weinbauern maßgefertigt. Besonders hervorzuheben ist die Wiederverwendung von Holz aus einer Scheune sowie von antiken Schränken und Arbeitsplatten des früheren Besitzers, der Pferdekutschen und Reitsportausrüstung herstellte.
Im Außenbereich wurden ländlich inspirierte Gärten geschaffen, die geschützte Ausblicke und Treffpunkte bieten, die sowohl im Sommer als auch im Winter genossen werden können.

Entourée de vignes et de chênes centenaires, cette maison des années 1970 est le fruit d'une rénovation complète réalisée par la décoratrice d'intérieur Rita Chan, le architecte paysagiste Rob Maday et l'architecte Dylan Henderson. La propriété comprend la maison principale, une maison d'amis, un bureau et un bâtiment abritant un appartement d'amis et une cave à vin. La nouvelle conception a apporté une nouvelle vie et une nouvelle apparence sans perdre l'architecture vernaculaire d'origine. Les concepteurs lui ont donné un style moderne et épuré, mais aussi rustique et naturel. L'environnement a été une source d'inspiration, c'est pourquoi la palette de couleurs comprend des tons neutres apaisants avec des touches de vert et de terre sur un fond blanc.
À l'intérieur, le vintage et le moderne coexistent. Les meubles ont été commandés à des artisans locaux liés aux vendanges. À noter la récupération du bois d'une grange et des anciens placards et plans de travail de l'ancien propriétaire qui fabriquait des voitures à cheval et des équipements équestres.
Dans les espaces extérieurs, des jardins d'inspiration rurale ont été créés, avec des vues protégées et des espaces de rencontre dont on peut profiter été comme hiver.

Rodeada de viñedos y robles centenarios, esta casa de 1970 es el resultado de una reforma integral de la interiorista Rita Chan, el arquitecto paisajista Rob Maday y el arquitecto Dylan Henderson. La propiedad incluye la casa principal, una casa de huéspedes, un despacho y una construcción con apartamento de invitados y bodega. El nuevo diseño aportó una nueva vida y apariencia sin haber perdido la arquitectura vernácula original. Los diseñadores imprimieron un estilo moderno y limpio, a la vez que rústico y natural. La inspiración ha sido el entorno, por lo que la paleta de colores asume los tonos neutros tranquilizantes con toques de verde y tierra sobre fondo blanco.
En el interior convive lo vintage con lo moderno. Las piezas del mobiliario las hicieron por encargo artesanos locales y vinculados a la vendimia. Destaca la recuperación de la madera de un granero y los antiguos armarios y encimeras del anterior propietario que fabricaba coches de caballos y equipamiento ecuestre.
En los espacios exteriores, se crearon jardines de inspiración rural, con vistas protegidas y espacios de reunión que se disfrutan tanto en verano como en invierno.

Floor plan

1. Auto court
2. Main house
3. Rain garden
4. Guest house
   and stables
5. Pool and spa
6. Al fresco dining
7. Garage

8. Office
9. Olive allée
10. Flowering meadow
    and orchard
11. Boutique vineyard
12. Sport court
13. Guest house
14. Shed

João Rodrigues, founder of Silent Living, inherited his family's entrepreneurial spirit, and combines his time as a hotelier with flying around the world as a professional long-haul pilot.

With five properties in Portugal, the small brand started with Casas Na Areia, the family's weekend home in Comporta, designed by his friend the Portuguese architect Manuel Aires Mateus and selected to represent Portugal at the Venice Biennale.

Architecture is central to the company's projects, which are represented by homes with a humble, homely approach to luxury. Rodrigues and Mateus share values in design, place, heritage and history. They represent the local and use materials close to the houses, respecting local craftsmanship.

João Rodrigues, der Gründer von Silent Living, hat den Unternehmergeist seiner Familie geerbt und kombiniert seine Rolle als Hotelier mit Langstreckenflügen als professioneller Pilot.

Mit fünf Immobilien in Portugal begann die kleine Marke mit dem Casas Na Areia, dem Wochenendhaus der Familie in Comporta, entworfen von seinem Freund, dem portugiesischen Architekten Manuel Aires Mateus, und ausgewählt, um Portugal auf der Biennale in Venedig zu repräsentieren.

Die Architektur spielt eine wesentliche Rolle in den Projekten des Unternehmens, das Häuser mit einem bescheidenen und gemütlichen Ansatz für Luxus schafft. Rodrigues und Mateus teilen Werte im Design, Ort, Erbe und Geschichte. Sie repräsentieren das Lokale und verwenden Materialien, die den Häusern nahe sind, und respektieren das lokale Handwerk.

© Matilde Travassos © Philippa Langley

SILENT LIVING

JOÃO RODRIGUES, AIRES MATEUS

silentliving.pt

João Rodrigues, fondateur de Silent Living, a hérité de l'esprit d'entreprise de sa famille et combine ses activités d'hôtelier avec ses vols autour du monde en tant que pilote professionnel de long-courrier.

Avec cinq propriétés au Portugal, la petite marque a commencé avec Casas Na Areia, la maison de week-end de la famille à Comporta, conçue par son ami l'architecte portugais Manuel Aires Mateus et sélectionnée pour représenter le Portugal à la Biennale de Venise.

L'architecture est au cœur des projets de l'entreprise, qui se caractérisent par des maisons dont l'approche du luxe est humble et familiale. Rodrigues et Mateus partagent des valeurs en matière de design, de lieu, de patrimoine et d'histoire. Ils représentent le local et utilisent des matériaux proches des maisons, en respectant l'artisanat local.

João Rodrigues, fundador de Silent Living, heredó el espíritu emprendedor de su familia, y compagina su faceta de hotelero con vuelos por todo el mundo como piloto profesional de avión de largo recorrido.

Con cinco propiedades en Portugal, la pequeña marca comenzó con Casas Na Areia, la vivienda familiar de fin de semana en Comporta, diseñada por su amigo el arquitecto portugués Manuel Aires Mateus y seleccionada para representar a Portugal en la Bienal de Venecia.

La arquitectura es esencial en los proyectos de la empresa que se caracteriza por casas con un enfoque humilde y hogareño del lujo. Rodrigues y Mateus comparten valores en diseño, lugar, patrimonio e historia. Representan lo local y utilizan materiales cercanos a las casas, respetando la artesanía local.

CASA NO TEMPO

Alentejo, Portugal

Photos © Nelson Garrido

The Alentejo region is known for its placid landscape and vast plains. Casa No Tempo stands as a timeless refuge in the midst of this rural landscape, as a witness to a family legacy that seeks to band together the past with the future. The owner, João Rodrigues, commissioned the renovation of the old farmhouse to his friend the architect Manuel Aires Mateus, under the guideline of combining rustic charm with modern comforts.
The house has spacious rooms offering views of the landscape. The floors are paved with local clay bricks. The kitchen is integrated into a white marble structure and the living room is light and airy. The four suites exude comfort and elegance, and the bathrooms feature walk-in showers and handmade tiles.
The property encompasses 1.000 acres of cork oak trees, pastures, wild fields, two dams, five ponds, streams and creeks. A 400 m² swimming pool, with a modern design and sand-coloured liner, blends perfectly into the pastures. In the pool area, parasols made from antique candle sets provide shade over comfortable day beds.

Die Region Alentejo ist bekannt für ihre ruhige Landschaft und weiten Ebenen. Casa No Tempo erhebt sich als zeitloser Rückzugsort inmitten dieser ländlichen Umgebung und ist ein Zeugnis des familiären Erbes, das Vergangenheit und Zukunft verbinden möchte. Der Besitzer João Rodrigues beauftragte den Architekten Manuel Aires Mateus mit der Renovierung des alten Landhauses mit dem Ziel, rustikalen Charme mit modernem Komfort zu vereinen.
Das Haus verfügt über geräumige Zimmer mit Blick auf die Landschaft. Der Boden ist mit lokalen Ziegelsteinen gepflastert. Die Küche ist in eine Struktur aus weißem Marmor integriert und das Wohnzimmer ist hell und geräumig. Die vier Suiten strahlen Komfort und Eleganz aus, und die Badezimmer sind mit bodenebenen Duschen und handgefertigten Fliesen ausgestattet.
Das Anwesen umfasst tausend Hektar Korkeichenwälder, Weiden, Wildblumenwiesen, zwei Dämme, fünf Teiche, Bäche und Bäche. Ein 400 Quadratmeter großer Pool mit modernem Design und sandfarbenem Belag fügt sich perfekt in die Wiesen ein. Im Poolbereich spenden Sonnenschirme aus alten Segelspielen Schatten auf bequemen Liegen.

La région de l'Alentejo est connue pour ses paysages tranquilles et ses vastes plaines. la Casa No Tempo est un refuge intemporel au milieu de ce paysage rural, témoin d'un héritage familial qui cherche à conjuguer le passé et l'avenir. Le propriétaire, João Rodrigues, a confié la rénovation de l'ancienne ferme à son ami l'architecte Manuel Aires Mateus, avec pour ligne directrice de combiner le charme rustique et le confort moderne.
La maison dispose de pièces spacieuses offrant des vues sur le paysage. Les sols sont pavés de briques d'argile locales. La cuisine est intégrée dans une structure en marbre blanc et le salon est clair et aéré. Les quatre suites respirent le confort et l'élégance, et les salles de bains sont dotées de douches à l'italienne et de carreaux faits à la main.
La propriété s'étend sur 1 000 acres de chênes-lièges, de pâturages, de champs sauvages, de deux barrages, de cinq étangs, de ruisseaux et de criques. Une piscine de 400 mètres carrés, au design moderne et au revêtement couleur sable, se fond parfaitement dans les pâturages. Dans l'espace piscine, des parasols fabriqués à partir d'anciens chandeliers offrent de l'ombre sur de confortables lits de jour.

La región de Alentejo es conocida por su paisaje tranquilo y sus vastas llanuras. Casa No Tempo se alza como un refugio atemporal en medio de este paraje rural, como testigo del legado familiar que busca unir el pasado con el futuro. El propietario, João Rodrigues, encargó la renovación de la vieja casa de campo a su amigo el arquitecto Manuel Aires Mateus, bajo la pauta de combinar el encanto rústico con las comodidades modernas.
La casa cuenta con amplias habitaciones que ofrecen vistas al paisaje. Los suelos están pavimentados con ladrillos de arcilla local. La cocina se integra en una estructura de mármol blanco y la sala de estar es luminosa y espaciosa. Las cuatro suites desprenden comodidad y elegancia, y los baños cuentan con duchas a ras de suelo y azulejos hechos artesanales.
La propiedad abarca mil acres de alcornoques, pastizales, campos salvajes, dos presas, cinco estanques, arroyos y riachuelos. Una piscina de 400 metros cuadrados, con un diseño moderno y revestimiento de color arena, se integra perfectamente en los pastizales. En el área de la piscina, las sombrillas hechas con juegos de velas antiguas brindan sombra sobre cómodas camas de día.

Founded in 1999 by Shannon Gaffney, Kyle Gaffney and Brian Collins-Friedrichs, the boutique design firm SkB Architects works on diverse projects around the world that feed and influence each other. For more than two decades, the Seattle-based studio has created meaningful environments rich in sensory stimulation for individual clients, corporate, retailers, developers and communities.

Through the buildings and spaces designed, SkB Architects strives to leave a positive mark on the world with humility, passion and optimism. With a holistic approach that encompasses architecture, interiors, lighting design, graphic communications and brand integration, the firm is dedicated to creating immersive experiences that engage all the senses.

SkB Architects, im Jahr 1999 von Shannon Gaffney, Kyle Gaffney und Brian Collins-Friedrichs gegründet, ist eine Boutique-Designfirma, die weltweit an verschiedenen Projekten arbeitet, die sich gegenseitig beeinflussen und bereichern. Seit mehr als zwei Jahrzehnten schafft das in Seattle ansässige Studio bedeutsame und sinnliche Umgebungen für individuelle Kunden, Unternehmen, Einzelhändler, Entwickler und Gemeinden.

Durch die von ihnen entworfenen Gebäude und Räume strebt SkB Architects an, mit Bescheidenheit, Leidenschaft und Optimismus einen positiven Einfluss auf die Welt zu hinterlassen. Mit einem ganzheitlichen Ansatz, der Architektur, Innenarchitektur, Lichtdesign, Grafikdesign und Markenintegration umfasst, widmet sich das Unternehmen der Schaffung immersiver Erlebnisse, die alle Sinne ansprechen.

SkB ARCHITECTS

STEVE OLSON, SHANNON GAFFNEY, KYLE GAFFNEY, DOUG MCKENZIE

skbarchitects.com

Fondé en 1999 par Shannon Gaffney, Kyle Gaffney et Brian Collins-Friedrichs, le bureau d'études SkB Architects travaille sur divers projets dans le monde entier, qui se nourrissent et s'influencent mutuellement. Depuis plus de vingt ans, le studio basé à Seattle crée des environnements significatifs et riches en stimulations sensorielles pour des clients individuels, des entreprises, des détaillants, des promoteurs et des communautés.

À travers les bâtiments et les espaces qu'il conçoit, SkB Architects s'efforce de laisser une empreinte positive sur le monde avec humilité, passion et optimisme. Avec une approche holistique qui englobe l'architecture, les intérieurs, la conception de l'éclairage, les communications graphiques et l'intégration de la marque, le cabinet se consacre à la création d'expériences immersives qui font appel à tous les sens.

Fundada en 1999 por Shannon Gaffney, Kyle Gaffney y Brian Collins-Friedrichs, la firma boutique de diseño SkB Architects, trabaja en diversos proyectos en todo el mundo que se retro alimentan e influyen mutuamente. Durante más de dos décadas, el estudio con sede en Seattle, ha creado entornos significativos y ricos en estímulos sensoriales para clientes individuales, corporativos, minoristas, desarrolladores y comunidades.

A través de los edificios y los espacios que diseña, SkB Architects se esfuerza por dejar una huella positiva en el mundo con humildad, pasión y optimismo. Con un enfoque integral que abarca la arquitectura, los interiores, el diseño de iluminación, las comunicaciones gráficas y la integración de marcas, la firma se dedica a crear experiencias inmersivas que involucran todos los sentidos.

SONOMA FARMHAUS

California, United States

Photos © Susanna Scott, Hannah Rankin

This house responds to the needs of an avid cyclist who was looking for a quiet place to gather with friends and family. The location was selected for its proximity to a small town and its community, as well as its accessibility by bicycle to Sonoma's picturesque landscapes.

The connection between the interior and exterior, both visually and physically, was a key aspect of the design. The aim was to create a space that is sober and harmonious with its surroundings, with structures that include a main dwelling, guest house, garage and bicycle storage, along with an outdoor community area with a fireplace and a large table. The materials used are adapted to the terrain, and have fire-resistant properties due to the risk of forest fires in the region. Solid rammed earth block walls, made from earth taken from the plot itself, support the structures. The house has an open-plan layout that allows a free flow between spaces. Minimalist furnishings have been chosen to eliminate visual distractions, while natural light filtered through a skylight softly illuminates the interior space.

Dieses Haus erfüllt die Bedürfnisse eines Amateur Radfahrers, der einen ruhigen Ort zum Treffen mit Freunden und Familie suchte. Die Lage wurde aufgrund der Nähe zu einem kleinen Dorf und seiner Gemeinschaft sowie der Fahrradzugänglichkeit zu den malerischen Landschaften von Sonoma ausgewählt.

Die Verbindung zwischen Innen- und Außenbereich, sowohl visuell als auch physisch, war ein Schlüsselelement im Design. Es sollte ein nüchterner Raum geschaffen werden, der im Einklang mit der Umgebung steht und Strukturen umfasst, darunter ein Hauptwohnhaus, ein Gästehaus, eine Garage und ein Fahrradlager sowie ein Gemeinschaftsbereich im Freien mit Kamin und großem Tisch. Die verwendeten Materialien passen sich dem Gelände an und sind aufgrund der Waldbrandgefahr in der Region feuerbeständig. Die massiven Wände aus Stampflehmziegeln, die aus dem eigenen Grundstück gewonnen wurden, bieten Unterstützung für die Strukturen. Das Haus verfügt über ein offenes Raumkonzept, das einen freien Fluss zwischen den Räumen ermöglicht. Es wurde minimalistisches Mobiliar gewählt, um visuelle Ablenkungen zu vermeiden, während das sanfte natürliche Licht durch ein Oberlicht den Innenraum sanft erhellt.

Cette maison répond aux besoins d'un cycliste amateur qui recherchait un endroit calme pour se réunir avec ses amis et sa famille. L'emplacement a été choisi pour sa proximité avec une petite ville et sa communauté, ainsi que pour son accessibilité à vélo aux paysages pittoresques de Sonoma.

Le lien entre l'intérieur et l'extérieur, à la fois visuel et physique, était un aspect clé de la conception. L'objectif était de créer un espace sobre et en harmonie avec son environnement, avec des structures comprenant une habitation principale, une maison d'amis, un garage et un local à vélos, ainsi qu'un espace communautaire extérieur doté d'une cheminée et d'une grande table. Les matériaux utilisés sont adaptés au terrain et présentent des propriétés ignifuges en raison du risque d'incendie de forêt dans la région. Les structures sont soutenues par de solides murs en blocs de pisé, fabriqués à partir de la terre prélevée sur le terrain lui-même. La maison a un plan ouvert qui permet une libre circulation entre les espaces. Un mobilier minimaliste a été choisi pour éliminer les distractions visuelles, tandis que la lumière naturelle filtrée par un puits de lumière illumine doucement l'espace intérieur.

Esta casa responde a las necesidades de un ciclista amateur que buscaba un lugar tranquilo para reunirse con amigos y familiares. La locación se seleccionó por su cercanía a un pequeño pueblo y su comunidad, así como por su accesibilidad en bicicleta a los pintorescos paisajes de Sonoma.

La conexión entre el interior y el exterior, tanto visual como física, fue un aspecto clave en el diseño. Se buscó crear un espacio sobrio y en armonía con el entorno, con estructuras que incluyan una vivienda principal, casa de invitados, garaje y almacén de bicicletas, junto con un área comunitaria al aire libre con chimenea y una amplia mesa. Los materiales utilizados se adaptan al terreno, y tienen propiedades resistentes al fuego debido al riesgo de incendios forestales en la región. Los sólidos muros de bloques de tierra apisonada, fabricados con tierra extraída de la propia parcela, brindan soporte a las estructuras. La casa presenta una distribución de planta abierta que permite un flujo libre entre los espacios. Se ha optado por un mobiliario minimalista para eliminar distracciones visuales, mientras que la luz natural filtrada a través de una claraboya ilumina suavemente el espacio interior.

Established in 2007, Smith Architects is a boutique design practice led by architect Stewart Smith. Renowned for their personalized and committed approach to the creative journey, the firm operates in both Brisbane and Byron Bay, crafting unique architectural and interior projects.
The practice takes pride in its capacity to intricately address the requirements of the occupants, fostering a profound connection between users and the surrounding environment. Smith Architects' direct experience on construction projects merge the two crafts of design and construction; this unique attribute significantly defines the essence of their work.

Smith Architects wurde 2007 gegründet und ist ein Boutique-Designbüro unter der Leitung des Architekten Stewart Smith. Das für seine persönliche und engagierte Herangehensweise an die kreative Reise bekannte Büro ist sowohl in Brisbane als auch in Byron Bay tätig und entwirft einzigartige Architektur- und Innenraumprojekte.
Das Büro ist stolz auf seine Fähigkeit, auf die Bedürfnisse der Bewohner einzugehen und eine tiefe Verbindung zwischen den Nutzern und der Umgebung zu schaffen. Die unmittelbare Erfahrung von Smith Architects bei Bauprojekten lässt die beiden Gewerke Design und Konstruktion miteinander verschmelzen; dieses einzigartige Attribut bestimmt maßgeblich das Wesen ihrer Arbeit.

SMITH ARCHITECTS

STEWART SMITH

smitharchitects.com.au

Fondé en 2007, Smith Architects est un cabinet de design dirigé par l'architecte Stewart Smith. Réputé pour son approche personnalisée et son engagement dans le processus créatif, le studio opère à la fois à Brisbane et à Byron Bay, où il produit des projets architecturaux et d'intérieur remarquables.
Le cabinet est fier de sa capacité à répondre précisément aux besoins des clients, en favorisant un lien profond entre les utilisateurs et l'environnement qui les entoure. L'expérience pratique de Smith Architects dans les projets de construction fusionne les aspects de la conception et de la construction de l'architecture ; cet attribut unique définit de manière significative l'essence de leur travail.

Fundado en 2007, Smith Architects es un estudio de diseño boutique dirigido por el arquitecto Stewart Smith. Reconocido por su enfoque personalizado y comprometido con el proceso creativo, el estudio opera tanto en Brisbane como en Byron Bay, donde elabora singulares proyectos arquitectónicos y de interiores.
El estudio se enorgullece de su capacidad para responder con precisión a las necesidades de los clientes, fomentando una profunda conexión entre los usuarios y el entorno que les rodea. La experiencia directa de Smith Architects en proyectos de construcción fusiona las vertientes del diseño y la construcción; este atributo único define significativamente la esencia de su trabajo.

THE FARMHOUSE + SHED

Queensland, Australia

Photos © Christopher Frederick Jones

After tilling the land alongside her family for 45 years, the owner of this house decided to construct a lifelong abode on the very plot they had nurtured. The architectural firm's mission was to pay homage to the profound memories and uphold the emotional bond woven between the land, its dwellers, and their shared experiences.
The design integrated the plough-carved textures, the dance of weather patterns, and the captivating interplay of sunlight and moonlight. Both the new house and shed were designed to nestle into the site, fostering a harmonious coexistence with the land. Natural materials took center stage, with exposed brick floors and eucalyptus timber carefully selected to echo the farm's distinctive characteristics. Elements reminiscent of the old shed and farmhouse were incorporated, evoking a sense of cherished nostalgia.
The orientation of the house provided both protection and engagement with the sun and wind. Mindful of the client's desire to age in place, the interiors discreetly embraced universal living features, offering seamless mobility for wheelchair users and ensuring stability moving around the spaces. A solar system and cross-ventilation pathways were thoughtfully installed, prioritizing the eco-friendly aspects of the design.

Die Eigentümerin dieses Hauses beschloss, ihr Haus auf dem Grundstück zu bauen, das sie mit ihrer Familie 45 Jahre lang bearbeitet hatte. Die Aufgabe der Architekten bestand daher darin, die Erinnerungen zu würdigen und die emotionale Verbindung zwischen dem Land, seinen Bewohnern und ihren gemeinsamen Erfahrungen aufrechtzuerhalten.
Sowohl das neue Haus als auch der Schuppen wurden so entworfen, dass sie sich in die Umgebung einfügen. Natürliche Materialien standen im Mittelpunkt, wobei freiliegende Ziegelböden und Eukalyptusholz ausgewählt wurden, um die charakteristischen Merkmale der Farm widerzuspiegeln. Es wurden Elemente eingebaut, die an den alten Schuppen und die Farm erinnern und ein Gefühl von Nostalgie hervorrufen.
Die Ausrichtung des Hauses bietet Schutz vor Sonne und Wind. Dem Wunsch des Bauherrn, an Ort und Stelle alt zu werden, wurde Rechnung getragen, indem die Innenräume für Rollstuhlfahrer zugänglich gemacht wurden. Um die Nachhaltigkeit zu unterstreichen, wurden eine Solaranlage und Querlüftungswege installiert, die den ökologischen Aspekten des Entwurfs Vorrang einräumen.

La propriétaire de cette maison a décidé de construire sa résidence sur la terre qu'elle a travaillée avec sa famille pendant 45 ans. La mission des architectes était donc de rendre hommage aux souvenirs et de maintenir le lien émotionnel entre la terre, ses habitants et leurs expériences partagées.
La nouvelle maison et la remise ont été conçues pour se fondre dans l'environnement. Les matériaux naturels ont été privilégiés : les sols en briques apparentes et le bois d'eucalyptus ont été choisis pour refléter les caractéristiques distinctives de la ferme. Des éléments rappelant l'ancien hangar et la vieille ferme ont été incorporés, évoquant un sentiment de nostalgie.
L'orientation de la maison protège du soleil et du vent. Tenant compte du désir du client de vieillir sur place, les intérieurs ont été conçus pour permettre aux personnes en fauteuil roulant de se déplacer. Pour mettre l'accent sur la durabilité, un système solaire et des voies de ventilation transversale ont été installés, donnant ainsi la priorité aux aspects écologiques de la conception.

La propietaria de esta casa decidió construir su morada en las tierras que había trabajado junto a su familia durante 45 años. La misión del estudio de arquitectos era por tanto rendir homenaje a los recuerdos y mantener el vínculo emocional entre la tierra, sus habitantes y sus experiencias compartidas.
Tanto la nueva casa como el cobertizo fueron diseñados para integrarse con el entorno. Los protagonistas fueron los materiales naturales con suelos de ladrillo visto y madera de eucalipto seleccionada para reflejar las características distintivas de la granja. Se incorporaron elementos que recordaban al antiguo cobertizo y a la granja, evocando un sentimiento de nostalgia.
La orientación de la casa protege del sol y el viento. Conscientes del deseo del cliente de envejecer en su lugar, los interiores incorporaron la movilidad para los usuarios de sillas de ruedas. Para hacer hincapié en la sostenibilidad, se instaló un sistema solar y vías de ventilación cruzada, dando prioridad a los aspectos ecológicos del diseño.

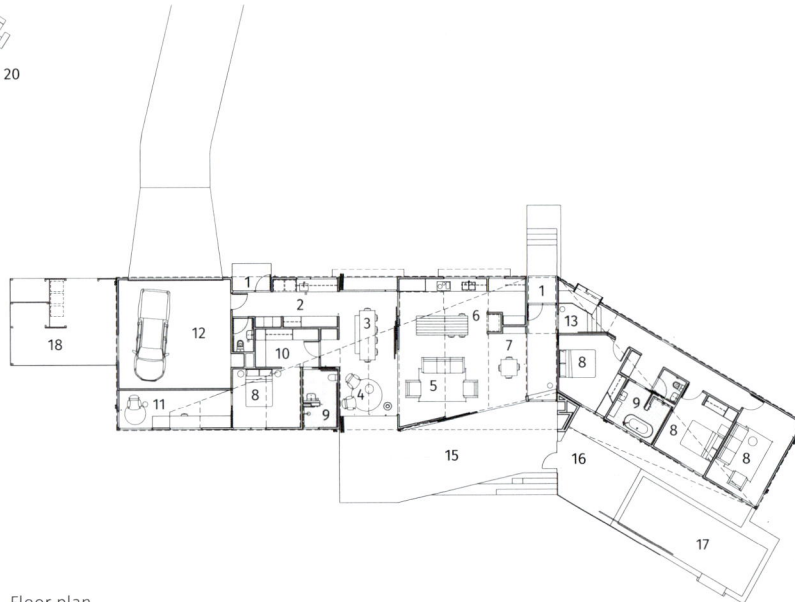

Floor plan

1. Entry
2. Mud/laundry
3. Dining room
4. Siting room
5. Living room
6. Kitchen
7. Eat
8. Bedroom
9. Bathroom
10. Robe
11. Study/sitting
12. Laundry
13. Reading
14. Playroom
15. Outdoor terrace
16. Pool terrace
17. Pool
18. Services enclosure
19. Shed
20. Tractor

Founded by Jeroen van Zwetselaar, this Bloemendaal-based firm specializes in global architecture and interior design projects. With a remarkable ability to establish a connection with each building, the firm creates spaces that convey a holistic feeling, as if they were intrinsically conceived. A fascination with contrasts is reflected in their designs, fusing the historic with the contemporary, as well as movement with serenity. The choice of earthy colors, natural materials and organic forms in his creations gives the works a peculiar and personal charm, while remaining in harmony with their surroundings. In addition, their approach focuses on the idiosyncrasies of each client, resulting in creations that exude an individual identity.

Das von Jeroen van Zwetselaar gegründete Büro in Bloemendaal hat sich auf globale Architektur- und Innenarchitekturprojekte spezialisiert. Mit einer bemerkenswerten Fähigkeit, eine Verbindung zu jedem Gebäude herzustellen, schafft das Büro Räume, die ein ganzheitliches Gefühl vermitteln, als wären sie von Grund auf erdacht worden. Die Faszination für Kontraste spiegelt sich in ihren Entwürfen wider, die das Historische mit dem Zeitgenössischen, die Bewegung mit der Gelassenheit verschmelzen. Die Wahl erdiger Farben, natürlicher Materialien und organischer Formen in seinen Kreationen verleiht den Werken einen besonderen und persönlichen Charme und steht gleichzeitig im Einklang mit ihrer Umgebung. Darüber hinaus konzentriert sich sein Ansatz auf die Eigenheiten jedes Kunden, was zu Kreationen führt, die eine individuelle Identität ausstrahlen.

STUDIO JEROEN VAN ZWETSELAAR

JEROEN VAN ZWETSELAAR

jeroenvanzwetselaar.com

Fondé par Jeroen van Zwetselaar, ce cabinet basé à Bloemendaal est spécialisé dans les projets globaux d'architecture et d'architecture d'intérieur. Avec une capacité remarquable à établir un lien avec chaque bâtiment, le cabinet crée des espaces qui transmettent un sentiment holistique, comme s'ils étaient intrinsèquement conçus. La fascination pour les contrastes se reflète dans leurs projets, fusionnant l'historique et le contemporain, ainsi que le mouvement et la sérénité. Le choix de couleurs terreuses, de matériaux naturels et de formes organiques dans ses créations confère aux œuvres un charme particulier et personnel, tout en restant en harmonie avec leur environnement. En outre, son approche se concentre sur les particularités de chaque client, ce qui se traduit par des créations qui dégagent une identité propre.

Fundada por Jeroen van Zwetselaar, esta firma con sede en Bloemendaal, se especializa en proyectos de arquitectura e interiorismo a nivel global. Con una notable habilidad para establecer una conexión con cada edificio, la firma crea espacios que transmiten una sensación holística, como si hubieran sido concebidos de manera intrínseca. La fascinación por los contrastes se refleja en sus diseños, fusionando lo histórico con lo contemporáneo, así como el movimiento con la serenidad. La elección de colores terrenales, materiales naturales y formas orgánicas en sus creaciones confiere a las obras un encanto peculiar y personal, mientras se mantienen en armonía con su entorno. Además, su enfoque se centra en la idiosincrasia de cada cliente, lo que da lugar a creaciones que destilan una identidad individual.

RIVERSIDE VILLA

Heemstede, The Netherlands

Photos © Kasia Gatkowska

Located in Noord Holland, on the banks of the Spaarne River, this house was originally built in 1900. In the decades that followed it underwent various additions and modifications that completely transformed it. However, no further changes had been made since the 1970s, which provided an excellent opportunity to restore its original details, bringing them up to today's standards.
The house had undergone so many renovations that restoring its lost character was an ideal challenge for Jeroen van Zwetselaar, whose premise was to create a design where the client would feel at home. To this end, the original archetype of the building was restored and an extension was added to the rear of the building to create a cozy living area. The design of the new extension is based mainly on large windows that open onto the garden, which in turn extends to the river. The incorporation of quirky nooks and crannies gives the house a certain air of imperfection that fits in with the signature style of the architecture. The burnt wood cladding on the facade pays homage to the old shipyards in the area.

Dieses Haus in Nordholland, am Ufer des Flusses Spaarne, wurde ursprünglich im Jahr 1900 erbaut. In den darauffolgenden Jahrzehnten wurde es mehrfach umgebaut und verändert, so dass es sich völlig verändert hat. Seit den 1970er Jahren wurden jedoch keine weiteren Veränderungen mehr vorgenommen, so dass sich eine hervorragende Gelegenheit bot, die ursprünglichen Details nach modernen Standards zu restaurieren. Das Haus hatte so viele Veränderungen erfahren, dass die Wiederherstellung seines verlorenen Charakters eine ideale Herausforderung für Jeroen van Zwetselaar darstellte, dessen Prämisse es war, ein Design zu schaffen, in dem sich der Kunde zu Hause fühlen würde. Zu diesem Zweck wurde der ursprüngliche Archetyp des Gebäudes wiederhergestellt und ein Anbau auf der Rückseite des Gebäudes errichtet, um einen gemütlichen Wohnbereich zu schaffen. Das Design des neuen Anbaus basiert hauptsächlich auf großen Fenstern, die sich zum Garten hin öffnen, der sich wiederum bis zum Fluss erstreckt. Die Einbindung eigenwilliger Ecken und Winkel verleiht dem Haus einen gewissen Hauch von Unvollkommenheit, der zum charakteristischen Stil der Architektur passt. Die Verkleidung der Fassade mit gebranntem Holz ist eine Hommage an die alten Werften in der Gegend.

Située dans le nord de la Hollande, sur les rives de la rivière Spaarne, cette maison a été construite en 1900. Au cours des décennies suivantes, elle a subi plusieurs ajouts et modifications qui l'ont complètement transformée. Cependant, aucune autre modification n'a été apportée depuis les années 1970, ce qui a fourni une excellente occasion de restaurer ses détails d'origine pour les mettre en conformité avec les normes modernes.
La maison avait subi tellement de modifications que la restauration de son caractère perdu était un défi idéal pour Jeroen van Zwetselaar, dont l'objectif était de créer un design dans lequel le client se sentirait chez lui. À cette fin, l'archétype original du bâtiment a été restauré et une extension a été ajoutée à l'arrière du bâtiment pour créer un espace de vie confortable. La conception de la nouvelle extension repose principalement sur de grandes fenêtres qui s'ouvrent sur le jardin, lequel s'étend à son tour jusqu'à la rivière. L'incorporation de coins et recoins originaux donne à la maison un certain air d'imperfection qui s'inscrit dans le style caractéristique de l'architecture. Le bardage en bois brûlé de la façade rend hommage aux anciens chantiers navals de la région.

Ubicada en Noord Holland, a orillas del río Spaarne, esta casa fue originalmente construida en 1900. En las décadas posteriores sufrió diversas adiciones y modificaciones que la transformaron por completo. Sin embargo, desde los años 70 no se habían realizado más cambios, lo que brindó una excelente oportunidad para restaurar sus detalles originales, adaptándolos a los estándares actuales.
La vivienda había experimentado tantas reformas que devolverle el carácter que había perdido resultó un desafío ideal para Jeroen van Zwetselaar, que contaba con la premisa de crear un diseño donde cliente se sienta como en casa. Para ello se recuperó el arquetipo original de la construcción y se hizo una ampliación en la parte trasera donde se configuró una acogedora zona de estar. El diseño de la nueva ampliación se basa principalmente en amplios ventanales que se abren hacia el jardín, el cual a su vez se extiende hasta el río. La incorporación de rincones peculiares confiere a la vivienda un cierto aire de imperfección que encaja con el estilo de firma de arquitectura. El revestimiento de la fachada en madera quemada rinde homenaje a los antiguos astilleros de la zona.

Sumich Chaplin Architects is a renowned residential architectural practice founded in 1984 by Lawrence Sumich, following his return from California. His innovative and creative approach is distinguished by creative and enduring architecture that responds to the surrounding context, landscape and environment. With a team of 16 staff, including two associate directors, the Auckland-based practice is noted for its attention to construction detail and exceeding expectations in design and functionality. The team works for national and international clients in a collaborative office environment, leveraging their experience and skills to create exceptional architecture.

Sumich Chaplin Architects ist eine renommierte Praxis für Wohnarchitektur, die 1984 von Lawrence Sumich gegründet wurde, nachdem er aus Kalifornien zurückgekehrt war. Ihr innovativer und kreativer Ansatz zeichnet sich durch dauerhafte und kreative Architektur aus, die auf die umgebende Umgebung, die Landschaft und die Umwelt reagiert.
Mit einem Team von 16 Mitarbeitern, darunter zwei Associate Directors, zeichnet sich die in Auckland ansässige Praxis durch ihre Aufmerksamkeit für konstruktive Details und die Erfüllung von Design- und Funktionalitätsansprüchen aus. Das Team arbeitet für nationale und internationale Kunden in einer kooperativen Büroumgebung und nutzt seine Erfahrung und Fähigkeiten, um außergewöhnliche Architektur zu schaffen.

SUMICH CHAPLIN ARCHITECTS

LAWRENCE SUMICH

sumichchaplin.com

Sumich Chaplin Architects est un cabinet d'architecture résidentielle renommé, fondé en 1984 par Lawrence Sumich, à son retour de Californie. Son approche innovante et créative se caractérise par une architecture créative et durable qui répond au contexte, au paysage et à l'environnement.
Avec une équipe de 16 personnes, dont deux directeurs associés, le cabinet basé à Auckland est réputé pour l'attention qu'il porte aux détails de la construction et pour sa capacité à dépasser les attentes en matière de conception et de fonctionnalité. L'équipe travaille pour des clients nationaux et internationaux dans un environnement de bureau collaboratif, mettant à profit son expérience et ses compétences pour créer une architecture exceptionnelle.

Sumich Chaplin Architects es una reconocida práctica de arquitectura residencial fundada en 1984 por Lawrence Sumich, tras su regreso de California. Su enfoque innovador y creativo y se caracteriza por una arquitectura creativa y perdurable, que responde al contexto circundante, el paisaje y el medio ambiente. Con un equipo de 16 empleados, incluyendo dos directores asociados, la práctica con sede en Auckland, se destaca por su atención al detalle constructivo y la superación de expectativas en diseño y funcionalidad. El equipo trabaja para clientes nacionales e internacionales en un entorno de oficina colaborativo, aprovechando su experiencia y habilidades para crear arquitectura excepcional.

CAMBRIDGE STUD RESIDENCE

Tamahere, New Zealand

Photos © Simon Devitt

Located in the rural town of Tamahere, this home that welcomes visitors to a thoroughbred horse farm adopts an aesthetic inspired by the surrounding stables. The design revolves around a solid axis, with a tree-lined driveway as the focal point.
The main structure divides the building along an axis, and the design elegantly separates the central public areas from the private ones. The common space has a kitchen, dining room, a trophy room and a bar. The side wings house rooms for visitors interested in buying horses, including discreet private accommodation for the owners. An outdoor transition area connects the main structure to the horses' grazing fields, creating a seamless connection to nature.
Throughout the lodge, skylights have been placed to allow filtered light to penetrate deep into the buildings and create a serene and welcoming atmosphere. The project is a testimonial to the team's expertise in harmony to architectural form with functional and aesthetic considerations, resulting in a seductive space with thoughtful interior design.

Dieses Haus in der ländlichen Gemeinde Tamahere empfängt Besucher einer Vollblutzucht und greift die Ästhetik der umliegenden Ställe auf. Das Design dreht sich um eine solide Achse, mit einem von Bäumen gesäumten Eingangsweg als Mittelpunkt.
Die Hauptstruktur teilt das Gebäude entlang einer Achse und das Design trennt elegant den zentralen öffentlichen Bereich vom privaten Bereich. Der Gemeinschaftsbereich umfasst Küche, Esszimmer, eine Trophäensammlung und eine Bar. Die seitlichen Flügel beherbergen Zimmer für Besucher, die an Pferdekäufen interessiert sind, einschließlich einer diskreten privaten Unterkunft für die Eigentümer. Ein Außenbereich verbindet die Hauptstruktur mit den Pferdeweiden und schafft eine nahtlose Verbindung zur Natur.
Im gesamten Haus wurden Oberlichter eingebaut, um ein sanftes, gefiltertes Licht tief in die Gebäude eindringen zu lassen und eine ruhige und einladende Atmosphäre zu schaffen. Das Projekt zeugt von der Erfahrung des Teams, architektonische Formen mit funktionalen und ästhetischen Überlegungen in Einklang zu bringen und einen ansprechenden Raum mit sorgfältigem Interior Design zu schaffen.

Située dans la ville rurale de Tamahere, cette maison destinée aux visiteurs d'une ferme de chevaux pursang adopte une esthétique inspirée des écuries environnantes. La conception s'articule autour d'un axe solide, avec une allée bordée d'arbres comme point central.
La structure principale divise le bâtiment le long d'un axe, et la conception sépare élégamment la zone publique centrale des zones privées. L'espace commun comprend une cuisine, une salle à manger, une salle des trophées et un bar. Les ailes latérales abritent des chambres pour les visiteurs intéressés par l'achat de chevaux, ainsi que des logements privés discrets pour les propriétaires. Une zone de transition extérieure relie la structure principale aux pâturages des chevaux, créant ainsi une connexion transparente avec la nature.
Dans tout le bâtiment, des puits de lumière ont été placés pour permettre à la lumière filtrée de pénétrer profondément dans les bâtiments et de créer une atmosphère sereine et accueillante. Le projet témoigne de l'expertise de l'équipe dans l'harmonisation de la forme architecturale avec des considérations fonctionnelles et esthétiques, ce qui a permis de créer un espace séduisant avec un aménagement intérieur bien pensé.

Situada en la localidad rural de Tamahere, esta casa que acoge a los visitantes de una granja de caballos de pura sangre adopta una estética inspirada en los establos circundantes. El diseño gira en torno a un eje sólido, con un camino de entrada bordeado de árboles como punto focal.
La estructura principal divide el edificio a lo largo de un eje, y el diseño separa elegantemente la zona pública central de las privadas. El área común tiene cocina, comedor, una sala de trofeos y un bar. Las alas laterales albergan las habitaciones para los visitantes interesados en comprar caballos, incluido un discreto alojamiento privado para los propietarios. Una zona exterior de transición conecta la estructura principal con los campos de pastoreo de los caballos, creando una conexión fluida con la naturaleza.
En toda la cabaña, se han colocado lucernarios para permitir que la luz filtrada penetre profundamente en los edificios y genere una atmósfera serena y acogedora. El proyecto es un testimonio de la experiencia del equipo en armonizar la forma arquitectónica con consideraciones funcionales y estéticas, lo que resulta en un espacio seductor con un cuidado interiorismo.

Sketch

Turkel Design has changed residential architecture with its innovative approach to modern prefabricated housing. Founded by Joel Turkel and Meelena Oleksiuk Turkel, who lead the practice alongside partner Jake Wright, the firm excels in the design and delivery of elegant premium homes. Creative lead Joel Turkel has overseen the design of over 200 modern prefabricated homes in North America and beyond. His commitment to innovation and efficiency has earned him the prestigious Marvin E. Goody Award. Meelena Oleksiuk Turkel is in charge of process development, marketing and interior design, having studied in Canada, Switzerland and the United States and earned a Master of Architecture from the Massachusetts Institute of Technology. Jake Wright, a summa cum laude Master of Architecture graduate from the State University of New York, is responsible for project oversight and business development and has been recognised with an NCARB Grand Award.

Turkel Design hat mit seinem innovativen Ansatz für moderne Fertighäuser die Wohnarchitektur verändert. Gegründet von Joel Turkel und Meelena Oleksiuk Turkel, die das Büro zusammen mit ihrem Partner Jake Wright leiten, zeichnet sich das Unternehmen durch die Gestaltung und Lieferung eleganter Premiumhäuser aus. Der kreative Leiter Joel Turkel hat das Design von über 200 modernen Fertighäusern in Nordamerika und darüber hinaus geleitet. Sein Engagement für Innovation und Effizienz hat ihm den renommierten Marvin E. Goody Award eingebracht. Meelena Oleksiuk Turkel ist für die Prozessentwicklung, das Marketing und die Innenarchitektur zuständig. Sie hat in Kanada, der Schweiz und den Vereinigten Staaten studiert und am Massachusetts Institute of Technology einen Master of Architecture erworben. Jake Wright, der seinen Master of Architecture an der State University of New York mit summa cum laude abgeschlossen hat, ist für die Projektaufsicht und Geschäftsentwicklung zuständig und wurde mit einem NCARB Grand Award ausgezeichnet.

TURKEL DESIGN

JOEL TURKEL, MEELENA OLEKSIUK TURKEL, JAKE WRIGHT

turkeldesign.com

Turkel Design a changé l'architecture résidentielle grâce à son approche innovante de l'habitat préfabriqué moderne. Fondée par Joel Turkel et Meelena Oleksiuk Turkel, qui dirigent le cabinet aux côtés de l'associé Jake Wright, l'entreprise excelle dans la conception et la livraison d'élégantes maisons haut de gamme. Joel Turkel, responsable de la création, a supervisé la conception de plus de 200 maisons préfabriquées modernes en Amérique du Nord et ailleurs. Son engagement en faveur de l'innovation et de l'efficacité lui a valu le prestigieux Marvin E. Goody Award. Meelena Oleksiuk Turkel est chargée du développement des processus, du marketing et de la décoration intérieure. Elle a étudié au Canada, en Suisse et aux États-Unis et a obtenu une maîtrise d'architecture au Massachusetts Institute of Technology. Jake Wright, titulaire d'une maîtrise d'architecture de l'Université d'État de New York, est responsable de la supervision des projets et du développement commercial. Il a reçu un Grand Award du NCARB.

Turkel Design ha revolucionado el concepto de la arquitectura residencial con su innovador enfoque de vivienda prefabricada moderna. Los fundadores Joel Turkel y Meelena Oleksiuk Turkel, dirigen el estudio junto con su socio Jake Wright. La empresa destaca en el diseño y la entrega de viviendas elegantes de primera calidad. Joel Turkel es el director creativo y ha supervisado el diseño de más de 200 casas prefabricadas en Norteamérica y otros países. Su compromiso con la innovación y la eficiencia le ha valido el prestigioso premio Marvin E. Goody. Meelena Oleksiuk Turkel se encarga del desarrollo de procesos, el marketing y el diseño de interiores. Estudió en Canadá, Suiza y Estados Unidos y obtuvo un máster en Arquitectura por el Instituto Tecnológico de Massachusetts. Jake Wright, graduado con un máster cum laude en Arquitectura por la Universidad Estatal de Nueva York, se encarga de la supervisión de proyectos y el desarrollo empresarial, y ha sido reconocido con un NCARB Grand Award.

MULMUR HILLS FARM

East Mulmur, Ontario, Canada

Photos © Maxime Brouillet

This house on 40 ha of land reflects the owners' admiration for the 19th century farm setting. Located next to a forest, it offers views of the barn, fields, pond and landscape of the Mulmur Hills. The design prioritises openness and connection to nature, with rooms opening onto the surrounding fields. The house serves as a retreat and part-time residence for a growing family, offering a warm and durable space for gatherings and celebrations. An exposed post and beam structure highlights the home's warm, natural materials, including sustainable, innovative wood products such as cross-laminated timber and thermally treated cladding. All structural materials were sourced and fabricated in Canada. Turkel Design's signature panelized prefab solution—in which the home is first designed using a 3D digital model, then assembled on a factory floor, and finally delivered as a building component package to the homeowners' land—reduced waste and assured a high level of quality in both materials and construction. Mulmur Hills Farm is refined and rustic, simple and open. It honors the rolling woodlands and agricultural heritage of the site while exemplifying the benefits of a forward-looking approach to both design and construction.

Das Haus liegt am Waldrand mit Blick auf eine Scheune, die Felder, den Teich und die Landschaft des Mulmur-Berge. Bei der Gestaltung des Hauses wurden Offenheit und Naturverbundenheit großgeschrieben, und die Räume öffnen sich zu den umliegenden Feldern. Das Haus dient als Rückzugsort und Teilzeitwohnsitz für eine wachsende Familie und bietet einen warmen und dauerhaften Raum für Zusammenkünfte und Feiern. Eine freiliegende Pfosten- und Balkenstruktur hebt die warmen, natürlichen Materialien des Hauses hervor, darunter nachhaltige, innovative Holzprodukte wie Brettsperrholz und thermisch behandelte Verkleidungen. Alle Baumaterialien wurden in Kanada beschafft und hergestellt. Die für Turkel Design charakteristische Fertigbauweise, bei der das Haus zunächst anhand eines digitalen 3D-Modells entworfen, dann in der Fabrik zusammengebaut und schließlich als Bauteilpaket auf das Grundstück der Hausbesitzer geliefert wird, reduzierte den Abfall und gewährleistete ein hohes Maß an Qualität bei Material und Konstruktion. Mulmur Hills Farm ist raffiniert und rustikal, einfach und offen. Sie ehrt die hügeligen Wälder und das landwirtschaftliche Erbe des Ortes und ist gleichzeitig ein Beispiel für die Vorteile eines zukunftsorientierten Ansatzes bei Design und Konstruktion.

Située à côté d'une forêt, cette maison offre une vue sur la grange, les champs, l'étang et le paysage des collines de Mulmur. La conception privilégie l'ouverture et la connexion avec la nature, les pièces s'ouvrant sur les champs environnants. La maison sert de lieu de retraite et de résidence à temps partiel pour une famille qui s'agrandit, offrant un espace chaleureux et durable pour les rassemblements et les célébrations. La structure à poteaux et poutres apparents met en valeur les matériaux naturels et chaleureux de la maison, y compris les produits du bois durables et innovants tels que le bois lamellé-croisé et le bardage traité thermiquement. Tous les matériaux structurels ont été achetés et fabriqués au Canada. La solution de panneaux préfabriqués – la maison est d'abord conçue à l'aide d'un modèle numérique en 3D, puis assemblée en usine et enfin livrée sur le terrain des propriétaires sous la forme d'un ensemble d'éléments de construction – a permis de réduire les déchets et de garantir un niveau élevé de qualité tant pour les matériaux que pour la construction. La ferme Mulmur Hills est raffinée et rustique, simple et ouverte. Elle rend hommage aux forêts vallonnées et au patrimoine agricole du site tout en illustrant les avantages d'une approche tournée vers l'avenir en matière de conception et de construction.

Situada junto a un bosque, esta casa ofrece vistas al granero, los campos, el estanque y el paisaje de las colinas Mulmur. El diseño prioriza la apertura y la conexión con la naturaleza, con habitaciones que se abren a los campos circundantes. La propiedad está diseñada como un sitio para el descanso y residencia a tiempo parcial para una familia. La estructura de postes y vigas a la vista resalta los materiales cálidos y naturales, incluidos productos sostenibles e innovadores como la madera laminada cruzada y el revestimiento tratado térmicamente. Todos los materiales estructurales se obtuvieron y fabricaron en Canadá. La solución de paneles prefabricados —en la que la casa se diseña con un modelo digital en 3D, luego se monta en una fábrica y, por último, se entrega como un paquete de componentes de construcción en la parcela— redujo los residuos y aseguró la alta calidad de los materiales. Mulmur Hills Farm es refinada y rústica, sencilla y abierta. Honra los bosques y el patrimonio agrícola, al tiempo que ejemplifica los beneficios de un enfoque con visión de futuro tanto en el diseño como en la construcción.

Based in Northern California, Wade Design Architects is an award-winning firm whose work focuses on private residences, specialty shops, wineries and hospitality projects. The firm was founded by principals Ani and Luke Wade in 2007 with the goal of creating thoughtful, crafted work through collaboration with both clients and builders.
Wade Design Architects has completed projects throughout the United States and internationally in Australia, Dubai, Saudi Arabia, Kuwait and Panama, and is best known for their work in rural California.

Wade Design Architects ist ein preisgekröntes Architekturbüro mit Sitz in Nordkalifornien, dessen Arbeit sich auf private Wohnhäuser, Spezialgeschäfte, Weingüter und Gaststättenprojekte konzentriert. Das Unternehmen wurde 2007 von den Geschäftsführern Ani und Luke Wade mit dem Ziel gegründet, durchdachte, handwerkliche Arbeiten in Zusammenarbeit mit Kunden und Bauherren zu schaffen.
Wade Design Architects hat Projekte in den gesamten Vereinigten Staaten und international in Australien, Dubai, Saudi-Arabien, Kuwait und Panama realisiert und ist vor allem für seine Arbeit im ländlichen Kalifornien bekannt.

WADE DESIGN ARCHITECTS

ANI WADE, LUKE WADE

wade-design.com

Basé en Californie du Nord, Wade Design Architects est un cabinet lauréat dont le travail se concentre sur des projets privés résidentiels, commerciaux, d'entrepôts et d'hôtellerie. Le cabinet a été fondé par Ani et Luke Wade en 2007 dans le but de créer des œuvres bien pensées et réalisées en collaboration avec les clients et les constructeurs.
Wade Design Architects a réalisé des projets dans l'ensemble des États-Unis et à l'étranger, en Australie, à Dubaï, en Arabie saoudite, au Koweït et au Panama, et est surtout connu pour son travail dans les régions rurales de Californie.

Con sede en el norte de California, Wade Design Architects es una firma galardonada cuyo trabajo se centra en proyectos de residencias privadas, comercios, bodegas y hostelería. La empresa fue fundada por Ani y Luke Wade en 2007 con el objetivo de crear obras bien planteadas y elaboradas en colaboración tanto con los clientes como con los constructores.
Wade Design Architects ha realizado proyectos en todo Estados Unidos y a escala internacional en Australia, Dubai, Arabia Saudí, Kuwait y Panamá, y es más conocido por su trabajo en la California rural.

CALISTOGA MODERN FARMHOUSE

California, United States

Photos © Suzanna Scott

The couple commissioned Wade Design to design a modern farmhouse with architecture that captures the incredible views of the adjoining vineyards and serves the landscape. The architectural team conceived a series of timber-clad gabled structures that are arranged around courtyards and terraces. The project includes the main house, a guest house, the pool house and a carport.
Aesthetically, the aim was to achieve serenity through sobriety, with architecture and interior elements. Respect for the natural environment defined the choice of materials: stained wooden beams reminiscent of the building's exterior, an exterior stone grid that runs uninterrupted in a straight line into the interior, and slender steel doors and windows that provide plenty of light and a contrasting focal point.
The interior design conveys a light and ethereal ambience with white walls and natural wood flooring and furniture. Overall, the design reflects a refined experience that connects indoor and outdoor living and suits its unique location.

Das Ehepaar beauftragte Wade Design mit dem Bau eines modernen Bauernhofs, der die unglaublichen Aussichten auf die angrenzenden Weinberge einfängt und dem Landschaft dienen soll. Das Architektenteam entwarf eine Serie von zweigiebligen Holzverkleidungen, die um Innenhöfe und Terrassen angeordnet sind. Das Projekt umfasst das Haupthaus, ein Gästehaus, ein Poolhaus und eine Garage.
Von ästhetischer Sicht war das Ziel, Serenität durch Schlichtheit sowohl in der Architektur als auch in den Innenräumen zu erreichen. Die Auswahl der Materialien wurde durch den Respekt vor der natürlichen Umgebung bestimmt: gefärbte Holzbalken, die an die Außenseite des Gebäudes erinnern, eine nahtlose Steinverkleidung, die sich geradlinig nach innen erstreckt, und schlank profilierte Stahltüren und -fenster, die viel Licht und einen Kontrastpunkt bieten.
Das Innendesign vermittelt eine leichte und luftige Atmosphäre mit weißen Wänden und natürlichen Holzböden und Möbeln. Insgesamt spiegelt das Design eine raffinierte Erfahrung wider, die das Leben im Inneren und im Freien des Hauses verbindet und sich perfekt an die einzigartige Lage anpasst.

Le couple a demandé à Wade Design de concevoir une ferme moderne dont l'architecture capturerait les vues incroyables sur les vignobles adjacents et servirait le paysage. L'équipe d'architectes a conçu une série de structures à pignons revêtues de bois, disposées autour de cours et de terrasses. Le projet comprend la maison principale, une maison d'amis, le pool house et un abri pour les voitures.
Sur le plan esthétique, l'objectif était d'atteindre la sérénité par la sobriété, tant au niveau de l'architecture que des éléments intérieurs. Le respect de l'environnement naturel a déterminé le choix des matériaux : des poutres en bois teinté qui rappellent l'extérieur du bâtiment, une grille extérieure en pierre qui s'étend de manière ininterrompue en ligne droite jusqu'à l'intérieur, et des portes et fenêtres élancées en acier qui apportent beaucoup de lumière et un point focal contrasté.
L'aménagement intérieur transmet une ambiance légère et éthérée, avec des murs blancs, des sols et des meubles en bois naturel. Dans l'ensemble, la conception reflète une expérience raffinée qui relie la vie à l'intérieur et à l'extérieur de la maison et qui convient à son emplacement unique.

La pareja de propietarios encargó a Wade Design una granja moderna con una arquitectura que capturara las vistas increíbles de los viñedos contiguos y estuviera al servicio del paisaje. El equipo de arquitectos concibió una serie de estructuras a dos aguas revestidas de madera que se organizan en torno a patios y terrazas. El proyecto incluye la casa principal, una casa de invitados, la casa de la piscina y un cobertizo para los coches.
Desde el punto de vista estético, el objetivo era lograr la serenidad a través de la sobriedad, con la arquitectura y los elementos interiores. El respeto por el entorno natural definió la elección de los materiales: vigas de madera teñida que recuerdan al exterior del edificio, un entramado de piedra exterior que discurre sin interrupciones en línea recta hacia el interior, y puertas y ventanas de acero de perfil fino que aportan mucha luz y un punto focal de contraste.
El interiorismo transmite un ambiente ligero y etéreo con paredes blancas, y suelo y muebles de madera natural. En conjunto, el diseño refleja una refinada experiencia que conecta la vida en el interior y el exterior de la vivienda y que se adapta a su ubicación única.

Weber Arquitectos has stood out in the architectural scene since 2002. The combination of the creativity and experience of its founder, Fernando Weber, with the innovative perspective of Anina Schulte-Trux, an interior architect and partner in the firm since 2004, has been key to its recognition.
With a long history in projects of diverse scales, the firm based in Mexico City has expanded its scope to encompass the construction and real estate development areas, offering a comprehensive approach to its clients.
The firm's innovative and high-quality work is recognized in prestigious specialized publications. Additionally, the firm has been awarded multiple times, including the AD-Iconos del Diseño Awards, Firenze Entremuros Award, Noldi Schreck Award, Interceramic Award, and AAI Award, among others.

Weber Arquitectos hat sich seit seiner Gründung im Jahr 2002 im Architekturbereich einen Namen gemacht. Die Kombination aus Kreativität und Erfahrung des Gründers Fernando Weber und der innovativen Perspektive von Anina Schulte-Trux, Innenarchitektin und Partnerin des Büros seit 2004, hat zu ihrer Anerkennung beigetragen.
Mit langjähriger Erfahrung in Projekten unterschiedlicher Größenordnung hat das in Mexiko-Stadt ansässige Unternehmen sein Tätigkeitsfeld erweitert, um Bau und Immobilienentwicklung abzudecken und seinen Kunden einen umfassenden Ansatz anzubieten.
Die innovative und hochwertige Arbeit des Büros wird in renommierten Fachpublikationen anerkannt. Das Unternehmen wurde mehrfach ausgezeichnet, darunter mit dem AD-Iconos del Diseño Award, dem Premio Firenze Entremuros, dem Noldi Schreck Award, dem Premio Interceramic und dem AAI Award.

WEBER ARQUITECTOS

FERNANDO WEBER, ANINA SCHULTE-TRUX

weberarquitectos.com

Depuis sa création en 2002, Weber Arquitectos a réussi à se démarquer sur la scène architecturale. La combinaison de la créativité et de l'expérience de son fondateur, Fernando Weber, avec la perspective innovante d'Anina Schulte-Trux, architecte d'intérieur et partenaire du cabinet depuis 2004, a été la clé de sa reconnaissance.
Forte d'une longue expérience dans des projets d'envergure variable, la société basée à Mexico a élargi son champ d'action à la construction et au développement immobilier, offrant ainsi une approche globale à ses clients.
Le travail innovant et de haute qualité de la société est reconnu dans des publications professionnelles prestigieuses. En outre, le cabinet a remporté plusieurs prix tels que l'AD-Iconos del Diseño, le Premio Firenze Entremuros, le Noldi Schreck, le Premio Interceramic et l'AAI, entre autres.

Weber Arquitectos ha logrado destacar en el panorama arquitectónico desde su fundación en 2002. La combinación de la creatividad y experiencia de su fundador, Fernando Weber, con la perspectiva innovadora de Anina Schulte-Trux, arquitecta de interiores y socia del despacho desde 2004, ha sido clave en su reconocimiento.
Con una larga trayectoria en proyectos de diversa escala, la firma con sede en Ciudad de México, ha ampliado su alcance para abarcar el área de construcción y desarrollo inmobiliario, y ofrecer un enfoque integral a sus clientes.
El trabajo innovador y de alta calidad del despacho es reconocido en prestigiosas publicaciones especializadas. Además, la firma ha sido galardonada en varias ocasiones como los premios AD-Iconos del Diseño, Premio Firenze Entremuros, Noldi Schreck, Premio Interceramic y AAI, entre otros.

TINY HOUSE

Valle de Bravo, State of Mexico, Mexico

Photos © Sergio López

This rest house embodies a simple and functional design. It is elevated from the ground on a platform with a metal structure that forms a terrace with panoramic views of the forest. Due to time and budget constraints, the challenge was to execute the project in a few weeks, which was made possible through the design's modularity and the use of prefabricated structure. The house is built with assembled thermally treated wood slats, anchored to the metal structure to create the walls.
Priority was given to the common area, while the bedrooms were designed with minimal but not uncomfortable dimensions. The height of the spaces was enforced with bunk beds, and the rooms were defined with an intermediate bathroom to provide privacy. An elongated piece of furniture for storage permeably divides the bedrooms from the common area. This creates a sense of openness and establishes a seamless transition between public and private spaces.
The roof of the house slopes towards the forest and opens up, creating a double-height terrace that becomes an extension of the living space, facilitating the transition between the interior and exterior.

Dieses Ferienhaus ist durch sein einfaches und funktionales Design gekennzeichnet. Es erhebt sich auf einer Plattform über dem Boden auf einem Metallrahmen, der eine Terrasse mit Panoramablick auf den Wald bildet. Aufgrund von Zeit- und Budgetbeschränkungen bestand die Herausforderung darin, das Projekt in wenigen Wochen umzusetzen, was durch die Modulbauweise und vorgefertigte Struktur ermöglicht wurde. Das Haus ist aus thermisch behandelten Holzlamellen gebaut, die miteinander verbunden und an den Metallrahmen angebracht sind, um die Wände zu bilden.
Der Gemeinschaftsbereich wurde priorisiert und den Schlafzimmern wurden minimale, aber dennoch komfortable Abmessungen gegeben. Die Höhe der Räume wurde mit Etagenbetten genutzt, und die Zimmer wurden durch ein Zwischenbad für Privatsphäre definiert. Ein langes Möbelstück zur Aufbewahrung trennt die Schlafzimmer durchlässig vom Gemeinschaftsbereich.
Dies schafft ein Gefühl von Offenheit und gleichzeitig Intimität. Das Tiny House bietet einen Rückzugsort inmitten der Natur und ist ein Beispiel für effizientes und nachhaltiges Design.

Cette maison de relaxation a un design simple et fonctionnel. Elle s'élève depuis le sol sur une plate-forme reposant sur une structure métallique, qui forme une terrasse offrant une vue panoramique sur la forêt. En raison de contraintes de temps et de budget, le défi consistait à exécuter les travaux en quelques semaines, ce qui a été possible grâce à la modulation de la conception et à la structure préfabriquée. La maison est construite à partir de lattes de bois traitées thermiquement et assemblées entre elles, qui sont ancrées à la structure métallique pour créer les murs.
La priorité a été donnée à l'espace commun et les chambres ont été laissées avec des dimensions minimales, mais pas inconfortables. La hauteur des espaces avec des lits superposés a été mise à profit et les chambres ont été définies avec une salle de bain entre les deux pour assurer l'intimité. Un meuble de rangement allongé sépare les chambres de l'espace commun. Cela crée un sentiment d'ouverture et établit une transition transparente entre les espaces publics et privés.
Le toit de la maison s'incline vers la forêt et s'ouvre, créant une terrasse à double hauteur qui devient une extension de l'espace de vie et facilite la transition entre l'intérieur et l'extérieur.

Esta casa destinada al descanso responde a un diseño sencillo y funcional. Se eleva del suelo sobre una plataforma en una estructura metálica, que se forma una terraza con vistas panorámicas al bosque. Debido a limitaciones de tiempo y presupuesto, el reto fue ejecutar la obra en pocas semanas, lo cual fue posible gracias a la modulación del diseño y la estructura prefabricada. La casa está construida con lamas de madera tratada térmicamente y ensambladas entre sí, que se anclan a la estructura metálica para crear las paredes.
Se dio prioridad al área común y se dejó a los dormitorios unas dimensiones mínimas, pero no incómodas. Se aprovechó la altura de los espacios con literas y las habitaciones se definieron con un baño intermedio para brindar privacidad. Un mueble alargado para el almacenamiento divide de manera permeable los dormitorios del área común. Esto crea una sensación de apertura y establece una transición perfecta entre los espacios públicos y privados.
El techo de la casa tiene una inclinación hacia el bosque y se abre, creando una terraza de doble altura que se convierte en una extensión del espacio habitable que facilita la transición entre el interior y el exterior.

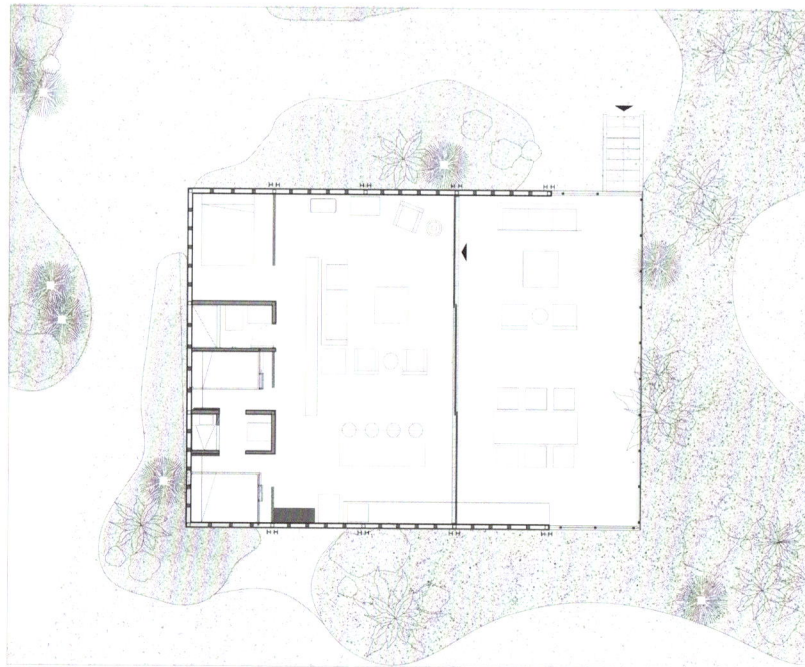

Floor plan